CARING
FOR YOUR
CAT

CARING
FOR YOUR
CAT

Paddy Cutts

Sebastian Kelly

This edition published in 1997 by
Sebastian Kelly
2 Rectory Road
Oxford OX4 1BW

© Anness Publishing Limited 1993

Produced by
Anness Publishing Limited

ISBN 1 901688 13 5

A CIP catalogue record for this book is available
from the British Library

Publisher: Joanna Lorenz
Senior Editor: Judith Simons
Editor: Lesley Ellis
Art Director: Peter Bridgewater
Designer: Annie Moss
Illustrator: Vana Haggerty

Printed in Singapore by Star Standard Industries Pte. Ltd.

1 3 5 7 9 10 8 6 4 2

CONTENTS

CAT
CHARACTERISTICS

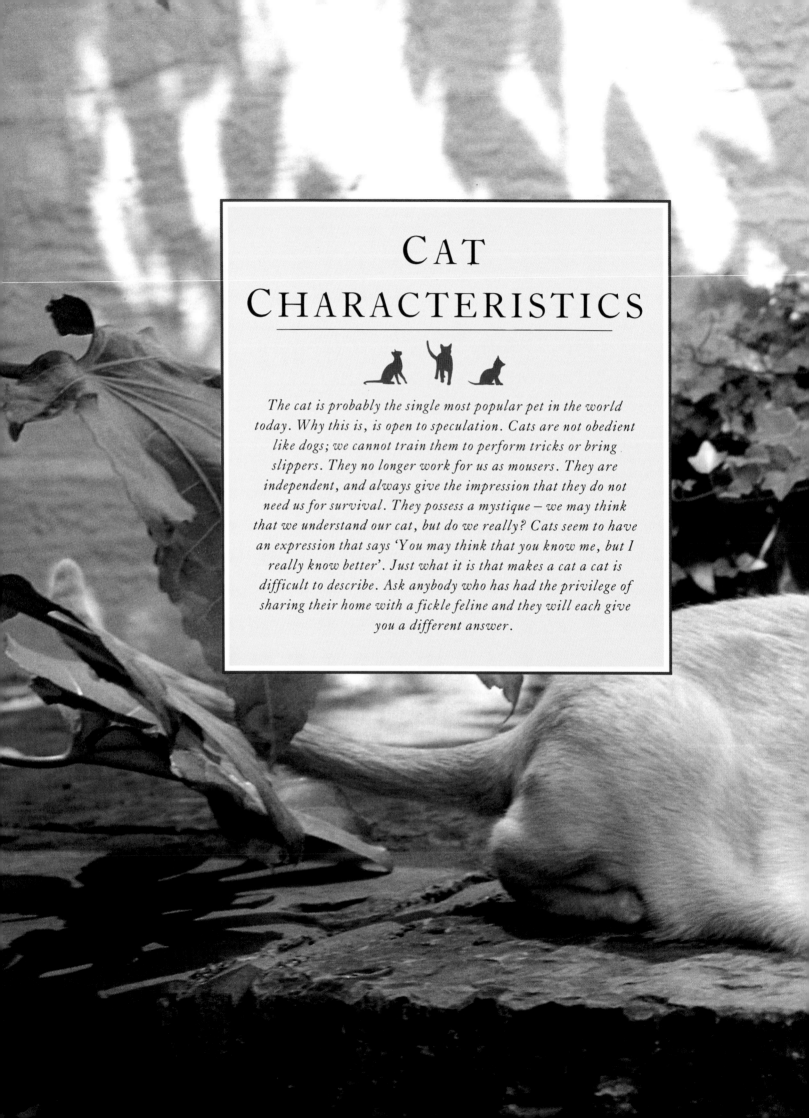

The cat is probably the single most popular pet in the world today. Why this is, is open to speculation. Cats are not obedient like dogs; we cannot train them to perform tricks or bring slippers. They no longer work for us as mousers. They are independent, and always give the impression that they do not need us for survival. They possess a mystique — we may think that we understand our cat, but do we really? Cats seem to have an expression that says 'You may think that you know me, but I really know better'. Just what it is that makes a cat a cat is difficult to describe. Ask anybody who has had the privilege of sharing their home with a fickle feline and they will each give you a different answer.

THE HISTORY OF
THE DOMESTIC CAT

Throughout history, the cat has been subject to several ups and downs in the popularity stakes.

Some of the earliest evidence of the domestic cat are to be found in Ancient Egypt, where it was worshipped as a god, and where the penalty for killing a cat was death. Cats were buried with the ceremony befitting a pharoah and it was common to mummify not just kings, but cats too. It is from these mummified felines that we have been able to learn much about the early domesticated cat. The British Museum in London holds

*The cat was a highly revered creature in Ancient Egypt as it was seen as the earthly embodiment of the cat goddess, Bast. Mummified remains reveal that this early domesticated cat sported a brownish ticked or tabby coat, as can be seen in these Egyptian wall paintings: a small cat crouches under a stool watching a chess-playing couple (**ABOVE**); a feline (**LEFT**) accompanies a family on a hunting expedition, flushing out fowl from the Nile marsh (from Thebes, c 1400 BC).*

booty from the raids carried out on pyramids at the turn of the century, including many mummified cats. When the bandages were removed, the cats were all found to be quite similar: small short-haired cats with brownish 'ticked' coats, rather similar to the breed we now call the Abyssinian.

Once worshipped as gods, the tide changed for the cat during the Middle Ages, when it was considered to be a witch's 'familiar'. Both witch and cat suffered the same fate, and were burned to death. The black cat has always been associated with witchcraft and from this, certain superstitions have arisen. A black cat crossing your path is supposed to be a bad omen, although some people in contrast consider a black cat to be a lucky mascot – wires have certainly got crossed somewhere along the line.

In Burma and Thailand, cats have always been held in high esteem. Breeds that we know today as Burmese, Siamese and Korat owe their ancestry to these far-off parts of the world. The Siamese was known as the 'Royal' Cat of Siam, and only royalty were allowed to own such a cat. It was considered an honour to be given one, and they were usually only bestowed on visiting dignitaries from

ABOVE
Cat with Fish; Indian Kalighat.

RIGHT
Kitten and Ball of Wool, by Murata Kokodu, 1866. This delightful Japanese painting shows a cat with the markings and short tail associated with the Japanese Bobtail breed.

LEFT
Yoshifuji, Witch Cat of Okabe on Tokkaido Road. This mischievous pair of cats show the classic mi-ke coloration of white, red and black.

variety of cat known as the Manx. It is thought that these tail-less cats first came to the island on ships from the Far East; stormy weather sometimes caused the ships to stop at the Isle of Man as they were unable to get into Liverpool, and it is quite likely that the occasional cat jumped ship here. As the island had little trading or contact with the mainland, these cats were free to breed only with each other and so the tail-less factor was increased. Even today, most cats on Man are tail-less, although they do produce the occasional tailed kitten.

variety of cat known as the Manx. It is thought that these tail-less cats first came to the island on ships from the Far East; stormy weather sometimes caused the ships to stop at the Isle of Man as they were unable to get into Liverpool, and it is quite likely that the occasional cat jumped ship here. As the island had little trading or contact with the mainland, these cats were free to breed only with each other and so the tail-less factor was increased. Even today, most cats on Man are tail-less, although they do produce the occasional tailed kitten.

THE EVOLUTION OF THE DOMESTIC CAT

All cats are descended from their larger, wild relations and some of this heritage can still be seen in the modern domestic cat, whether pedigree or moggie.

Evolution has given the cat a camouflaged coat so that it is hidden from predators. In the wild, the cat's natural instinct is to sleep by day and hunt under cover of darkness. A visit to the zoo will confirm just how successful this camouflage has been: lions, living in dry regions with sparse vegetation, have adopted a sandy colour to their coat; snow leopards are pale to blend with their snowy environment; jungle cats are usually spotted or striped, echoing the dappled light that illuminates the forest floor. Just as clever is the coat of the domestic tortoiseshell cat – for a female rearing her young, a camouflaged coat is important, and a tortie pattern makes her almost indistinguishable from the background in a variety of locations. The tortoiseshell gene is sex-linked for this purpose, occurring usually only in female cats.

. As cats tend to sleep by day, they have evolved another mechanism as well as coat colour to defend themselves, and this can still be seen in the domestic cat today. Cats have very little fur between the top of their eyes and their ears. Look at a cat

Continued page 13

ABOVE
The Manx is one of the best known of the tail-less varieties of pedigree cat. Indigenous to the Isle of Man, off the west coast of England, and popular worldwide, this breed has evolved through a limited gene pool restricted to the cat population of this remote island.

other countries who had won favour with the king. Perhaps because of the limited gene pool available in such remote regions these cats often had deformed tails.

Similar inbreeding was seen in Japan; isolated on an island, the indigenous cat population did not have the chance to mate with unrelated cats and so any fault in the genetic make-up would have been doubled up with each generation. This gave rise to the breed we now call the Japanese Bobtail.

As ships became larger, and were able to travel farther afield, this changed the cat's future. Cats were good mousers and most ships employed the services of a 'ship's cat'. Cats have always been excellent escapologists and it was not unknown for one to jump ship, which meant that the ship would then have to pick up a local cat as a replacement, and bring it back home.

Off the west coast of England, near the port of Liverpool, is the Isle of Man, a small island which is home to a tail-less

In the wild, camouflage is all-important to conceal animals from predators. Domestic cats, as well as their larger wild cousins, display coat patterns and colours designed to blend into their natural habitats. This tortoiseshell is almost imperceptible against the surroundings of the garden.

This sleeping Burmese cat gives the appearance of being awake, even though the eyes are tightly shut. The thin patches of fur immediately above the eyes will confuse a predator into thinking that the cat is alert and on guard.

WILD CATS

A sk any cat owner why they choose to share their life with a domestic feline, and the answer is often that they admire the cat's independent streak. This trait can be directly related back to its wild cat ancestry, that self-sufficient, superbly designed creature that has adapted itself to life in all corners of the world; hot or cold climates, snow or sun, rain forest or desert, mountain or flat land, there has always been a feline of some description that has adapted to the environment.

LEFT
The kittens of the Indian Desert Cat show distinct spots, but these fade in maturity.

BELOW
The Scottish Wild Cat has developed a thick, waterproof coat as a protection against harsh weather, and a fearsome expression to ward off predators.

LEFT
The name Jungle Cat is a slight misnomer as the cat originally evolved in the sandy area of Egypt, and has a pale, ticked coat colour suitable for camouflage in desert regions.

RIGHT
Leopard Cat is the common term for the La-Lang cat. The natural habitat for the species is dark forests and regions of long grass, hence the need for large eyes, and the spotted coat reflects the natural dappled light pattern that would fall on the forest floor.

ABOVE
The Siamese originates from the warm tropics and its typical smooth, silky and light-coloured coat allows the cat to cool quickly in extreme heat.

ABOVE
Burmese are an adaptable and sturdy breed. The very first Burmese did indeed come from Burma, but today they are quite acclimatized to the more severe winters of northern regions.

BELOW
The ever-popular Persian was first seen in the northern upland regions of Iran. With freezing temperatures at night and during winter, cats from this area needed thick coats to help keep them warm.

(Archangel'sk), have a curious 'double' coat, to keep them warm in Baltic climes.

Cats have been imported and exported for many decades and so do not always end up living in a climate suited to their type of fur. It is for this reason that owners of longhaired cats in tropical regions sometimes clip the long fur down during the hotter parts of the year, and that varieties from the Far East living in cooler areas benefit from additional heating during the cold seasons.

when it is asleep, and the bald area gives the impression of open eyes, so that any predator will think the cat is wide awake, on guard and ready to attack. It is a simple, but effective, form of protection.

The length and type of fur depends on which part of the world the cat originates from. The Scottish Wild Cat has a thick, dense coat which keeps it warm and dry in the bleakest of Scottish winters. Persians and Angoras, native to the upland regions of Iran and Turkey, developed long coats for the same reason; mountainous regions get cold at night and in the winter, and the extra long coat has an insulating effect. Pale-coated Siamese have a fine silky texture to their coat allowing them to cool rapidly when the weather is hot. Russian Blues, originally thought to have come from Archangel

• CAT BEHAVIOUR •

Much of the behaviour that the modern domestic cat displays directly relates to its wild origins. This is not always socially acceptable, but cats are

LEFT
A family unit of mother, father and daughter engage in social grooming. The male cat is showing friendly, paternal interest in the kitten but the situation could be quite different if this had been an intruding tom cat.

very territorial and much of what they do reflects their need to stake out territory, especially if they are not neutered.

In the wild, this territorial behaviour is important. In times of famine or drought, there is little food to go around and the male stakes out territory to ensure that intruders do not come and raid his particular area of available prey. If he has a female with kittens this is even more important, if the kittens are to survive. It is not unknown for a male cat to attack the young of another cat. This is still true today – a maurauding tom cat can easily kill a defenceless young kitten in your own back garden.

Cats like to mark out their territory with chemical messages; these tell any other cat that strays into the area to 'keep off'. The most common way of marking

LEFT
The Norwegian Forest Cat is endowed with a thick warm coat to protect it from the harsh winters of its native homeland in northern Scandinavia; it is also an excellent climber, even by feline standards.

BELOW
The most obvious way for a cat, particularly a male, to mark its territory is by spraying on it, as this Siamese stud cat demonstrates quite clearly.

ABOVE
Cats like to mark their 'property' with scent, which can be done in many ways. Glands behind the cat's ears will exude a smell particular to the cat, but imperceptible to humans. In this case the resident human has been considered worthy of being 'marked' in this way!

is by spraying concentrated urine around the boundaries of the territory. To humans, this is one of the most unpleasant smells we know and is usually associated with the entire male; another good reason for neutering. However, entire females – especially when on call – and even some neutered cats, will also spray. Cats that have been confined indoors during the cold winter months will probably spray all four corners of the garden when they are allowed out in the spring. Frost will have destroyed any trace of the previous territorial markings, and so the cat has to 'beat the bounds' of his territory before another cat lays claim to his patch.

As long as this activity is confined to the outdoors, it does not affect us too much; it is only when a cat starts to spray inside the house that it becomes socially unacceptable for us, although it makes perfect sense to the cat. It is not common for the well-adjusted, socially integrated and neutered cat to spray indoors, but it can happen.

The most common reason for a cat to spray indoors is when another feline is introduced to the household. The resident

cat sees it as a threat and will mark out 'his' home with his own personal scent. This can even happen if a piece of secondhand furniture is brought into the house that smells of another cat; the resident cat's instinct is to spray it just to be sure that it is adequately marked as part of his own home.

Cats also mark territory and leave chemical messages in other, more acceptable, ways. The cat has glands that secrete scent in several parts of their bodies, particularly around the back of the head. When a cat comes and rubs its head against your leg, it is actually marking you; the message it leaves is for other cats, and translates roughly as 'This is my human; keep away'. For the same reason, cats rub against domestic objects such as

LEFT
Even the domesticated entire male will feel the need to patrol its territory, often spraying to warn other male cats to keep away from its 'patch'.

ABOVE
Cats have scent glands in their paws, too, and when stropping a tree to sharpen their claws, they will be leaving messages for other cats at the same time.

furniture; they are marking their possessions, but in an inoffensive way.

The same behaviour can be seen outside in the garden, but takes more the part of a conversation between neighbouring cats as they leave messages for each other in a kind of 'dead letter box'. Rubbing against walls, trees and fences the cat can let the local feline population know what is going on: 'Susie' is on call at the moment or 'Sam' has just been neutered . . . . Even when a cat strops a tree to sharpen its claws, it leaves behind a message that comes from glands situated between the paw pads.

Male cats prowl, especially at night, calling for a female; the female on call will make just as much, if not more, noise. It is during these nocturnal forays

BELOW
This cat is picking up a 'message' which another cat has left on the wall.

◉ BODY LANGUAGE ◉

An intimidated or frightened cat will try to make itself look larger in front of the aggressor by fluffing up its coat, particularly the tail.

A cat on the attack will adopt an aggressive stance: whiskers bristle, muscles are taut, and the cat is lying low ready to pounce.

A cat that rolls over and exposes the most vulnerable part of its anatomy, the stomach area, is submitting to the aggressor.

◊ HUNTING INSTINCTS ◊

Crouching low, the cat surveys its prey.

Stealthily, the cat edges nearer.

Suddenly rising up, the cat pounces, ready for the kill.

Mission accomplished, and the cat has caught the mouse.

that a cat is most likely to get into a fight with another, as both are out looking for the same thing – a female to mate. In order to keep peace with the neighbours, and avoid expensive visits to the vet, most owners decide to neuter any cat that is a family pet and keep it in at night.

THE CAT IN THE HOME TODAY

Although we consider the cat to be a domesticated pet, this is not really so. No matter what restrictions we impose on our pets, they are still essentially cats and will always display a certain amount of wild cat behaviour. We can neuter them, keep them safely confined indoors and well fed, but they will still have the roaming instinct, and will want to hunt and catch prey even if they have just finished a meal. This is something that we cannot change; ask any cat lover and, if they answer honestly, they would not want to change it. Part of the charm of living with a cat is that it is probably the nearest most of us will ever get to sharing our home with a small, wild creature. If you want an obedient, well-behaved, dependable and loyal follower, choose a dog. If you want a lifelong friend that chooses you, will offer companionship and sense your every mood instinctively, while still retaining an independent streak, then a cat is for you.

RIGHT
*Cats are very much
creatures of habit and
believe in a serious
afternoon 'siesta'
during the hotter
months; this sensible
cat has chosen a shady
area for a snooze.*

LEFT
*The feline species is
fastidious and a large
part of a cat's day is
spent grooming in
order to keep its coat
in pristine condition.*

CAT SENSES

As natural nocturnal hunters, cats have evolved their sense organs to a highly tuned degree. Not only do these senses serve to aid hunting, but also to keep the cat safe from predators. Even though most cats today live in a safe, domestic environment, they still display many characteristics that they developed when the need to hunt for food and day-to-day survival was an important part of their lifestyle.

BELOW
In bright light a cat's pupils will contract to the narrowest of slits. Equally, in dim light they can dilate to a much greater degree than in humans, allowing cats to see better in low light levels.

◦ SIGHT ◦

It is not true that cats can see in the dark; with no illumination they can see no better than we can. However, it is true to say that they can see better than humans in low light levels. The feline eye is constructed differently to a human one: the eyeball is rounder with the lens and cornea closer to the retina, allowing the cat to focus more closely than we can; the pupil is capable of dilating to a much greater degree, so admitting more light to the retina and enabling the cat to see better in dim light; and the location of the eyes, which are set wider apart than ours, allows the cat a wider field of vision.

◦ HEARING ◦

Although the size of the feline ear varies considerably, they are always set on the head, rather than on either side of the face like humans and monkeys. The external ear organ, the pinna, is movable allowing for directional location of sound. The inner ear has larger echo chambers, so the cat can detect sounds imperceptible to humans, such as those emitted on very high and low frequencies.

BELOW
Set on the head rather than either side of the face, the cat's ears are movable allowing for directional location of sound. The pinna, or external ear, varies in size and is quite large in the Siamese breed.

● PURRING ●

How, and why, cats purr is debatable; in truth, nobody has scientifically discovered the whys and wherefores of this distinctly feline phenomenon. However here are some ideas.

It is thought that the cat's purr is the result of an electrical impulse generated by the brain, transferred to and carried by the central nervous system, causing certain muscles, particularly those located near the voice box, to contract and thus resonate. The end product, the purr, is felt as a vibration throughout the body but is particularly audible from nose and mouth.

As to why cats purr, this is a different story and these are some theories:

● *It helps increase the efficiency of the circulatory system, and so keeps the cat healthy.*

● *A soft purr is a demand, and a loud one a thank-you message to indicate that the cat has received what it wanted, usually food!*

● *It is a reassuring signal from mother to kitten.*

● *It is a signal from kitten to mother that all is well.*

● *A dominant cat will purr at a subservient one to show that it is not on the attack.*

● *Cats purr when frightened or about to be attacked to say that they are small, defenceless creatures that pose no threat.*

● *Sick, ill or injured cats purr to comfort themselves and to tell others that they are poorly.*

● *The purr is an indication of a pleasured, happy, content cat; this is probably the most popular reason for the purr, an answer most cats would agree with. Purr, and your owner will most likely give you what you want, even if it is the last prawn on the dinner table – cats are not stupid.*

● SCENT ●

The feline nose has olefactory receptors, extremely specialized organs, that can detect minute or extremely low concentrations of substances in the air. They transmit the information they receive to the olefactory lobes in the brain where the scents are recognized and acted upon. The olefactory lobes in animals are physically bigger, pro rata, than in man where they are almost vestigial.

● FLEHMING ●

Flehming is a reaction seen in many mammals. It causes the lips to curl back thus allowing more chemical aromas to register in the Jacobson's Organ. This is situated in the roof of the mouth and, in wild cats, affords the cat an additional method of knowing the 'lie of the land' and what other, possibly predatory, animals lurk nearby. In the domestic cat, this is not of such vital importance as with its wild brethren, and so the flehming reaction is not so obvious.

ABOVE
A cat on the prowl uses its refined sense of smell to locate scents left by other cats.

LEFT
'Flehming' is a reaction whereby the cat curls its lips back to absorb certain chemical aromas and scents, left by other cats, more efficiently into the Jacobson's organ. This is situated in the roof of the mouth and is lined with olefactory cells connected to the part of the brain concerned with sexual behaviour and appetite.

WHERE TO FIND A CAT – AND HOW TO CHOOSE ONE

Pedigree or non-pedigree, kitten or adult, rescue or purposely bred, longhair or shorthair, coat colour and pattern – which to choose? If owning a cat is your ideal, the possibilities are almost endless. Remember, your final choice of cat is a life-long commitment, so please consider this chapter seriously before making your decision.

ABOVE

*Cute, fluffy kittens
mature into full-
grown adults all too
soon and responsible
ownership entails both
time and effort.
Longhaired Persians
are attractive cats and
make affectionate
family pets, but their
long coats require
daily grooming.*

RIGHT

*Once away from its
mother, even a
shorthaired kitten will
benefit from a regular
grooming session with
its new owner.*

efore making a firm decision to buy a cat do bear the following in mind. Remember that a cat is a life-long undertaking; it can live for twenty years or more – as long as most children stay in the parental 'nest'. Most people think seriously before starting a family, and the adoption of a cat should also be considered very carefully. That cute, fluffy kitten bought on the spur of the moment will soon grow into an adult. It will need annual inoculations, spaying or neutering at about six to nine months, and possible veterinary treatment for illness. There is no free medical care for cats; some charities will help out in deserving cases, but basically think of your veterinary surgeon as a fairly expensive private doctor.

You will also probably want to take holidays and good boarding catteries are not cheap. Two English friends of mine with eight cats used to visit their son in Australia each year; they saved enough for the price of three return tickets, as the cost of boarding their cats amounted to a return trip to Sydney from London. If cost alone has not put you off the thought of sharing your life with a cat, read on.

All cats require grooming, but especially if they are longhaired. This takes time. Shorthaired cats benefit from a regular brush and comb, but longhairs need grooming for at least fifteen minutes a day to prevent the fur becoming tangled. This applies to non-pedigree cats as well as their more aristocratic relations.

It is very tempting to give in to children, especially at Christmas, and agree to give a kitten as a present. These kittens too often become the abandoned felines taken in to rescue centres in the New Year. The decision to share your home with a cat should be made only after a full family discussion. Consider who will clean the litter tray, feed the cat, be responsible for it, and pay the bills.

The Canine Defence League, in the UK, provides bumper stickers which read 'A puppy is for life, not just for

CATS AND THE ELDERLY

Cats can have a most therapeutic effect on their owners, especially if they are elderly. The cat's soothing purr, encouraged by gentle stroking, is known to lower the blood pressure and thus prevent heart problems. Constantly demanding, the cat will help to keep an older person active and make him or her get up out of the chair and prepare a suitable feline repast!

BELOW

If it is not important for your family to have a kitten, think seriously about taking in an adult rescue. It may take a little longer to settle in, as it will be more set in its ways, but will reward you with its friendship and companionship.

Christmas'. This should also be the motto for kittens: *never* give a kitten as a present to somebody without consulting them first; they may well like other people's cats, but might not want the responsibility of a pet of their own.

If by now you are not completely put off by the moral responsibility and indeed the expense of owning a pet, you must now decide what sort of cat you want: pedigree or non-pedigree, adult or kitten. There are many responsible ways to acquire a cat so, *if* you have firmly decided that you want one, consider the possibilities.

First, a word of warning. The most obvious place to buy a new pet would seem to be the local pet store. But, although pet stores are ideal for providing all the accoutrements for your new feline friend, they are hardly the right environment for a creature to grow up in. Pet shop kittens are likely to have been taken away from their mother too early and may be offered for sale when they are not even old enough to be wormed or to have the necessary inoculations. This makes them particularly vulnerable to

ABOVE

Cats and children can make ideal companions. However, before purchasing a cat or kitten, it is important that the whole family is aware of the responsibilities and duties involved.

any infectious illness, and could result in expensive vet's bills, and even death. Pedigree kittens in pet shops are usually the result of greedy breeders over-breeding their stock. No reputable cat breeder would even consider selling to a pet shop.

NON-PEDIGREE KITTENS

Moggies come in such a multitude of shapes, sizes, patterns, colours and varying length of fur that you can be spoiled for choice. Many can look extremely glamorous and, as their parentage is often unknown, may have a pedigree cat in their background.

The most obvious way to find a kitten is by word of mouth. In the summer months there are usually kittens looking for new homes but, fortunately, not as

ONE KITTEN OR TWO?

Consider your living and working arrangements. Is the home unoccupied for most of the day, or is there usually somebody at home? No young creature likes to be left on its own all day so, if you are out at work for any length of time, think about getting two kittens which will be company for each other. If you have to board them when you take a holiday, they will give each other companionship. A bored kitten may attack the carpets and curtains while you are at work, not to mention the houseplants and ornaments; two kittens will play with each other and spare you the expense of refurnishing your house and replacing valuables. You would hardly expect a human toddler to behave perfectly, so why expect more of a kitten?

For owners who are out at work all day but still wish for a cat, the sensible and responsible choice is to take two kittens, preferably from the same litter (ABOVE).

They will feel less nervous when introduced to their new home and will be companions for each other as they grow up (BELOW).

Non-pedigree cats come in a multitude of colours, fur lengths and coat patterns. Sleek black cats (**RIGHT**) *are always popular and highly sought-after, while this little odd-eyed white, auburn and tortie kitten* (**OPPOSITE**) *has instant appeal.*

*Kittens develop quickly and even within a few weeks look quite different. At eight weeks old (**RIGHT**), the soft, fluffy kitten coat and babyish expression is apparent, but only four weeks later (**FAR RIGHT**) the kitten looks far more like a small version of the adult cat it will become. At twelve weeks old the kitten is ready for its inoculations.*

many as there used to be. Some rescue organisations now offer subsidized neutering through a local vet and, in some cases, may even pay the whole bill. These schemes have been devised to try and control the population of unwanted cats, and in consequence there are fewer moggie kittens available to the responsible buyer. Other good sources are local papers which carry a 'pets for sale' column, and local cat clubs and cat charities which will also know of any kittens needing a home, as will most veterinary practices.

The age at which a non-pedigree cat goes to its new home will vary, but should certainly never be less than eight weeks. By this time the kitten, although not completely self-sufficient, is old enough to stand on its own four paws. But it will no longer have the immunity to infections that it received while suckling its mother's milk, as this contained protective antibodies, so from the age of six weeks the kitten is at its most vulnerable as it has no protection from disease, and twelve weeks is the earliest age that most veterinarians will administer the all important inoculations. However, it is reasonably safe to allow an eight-week-old to go to a new home that does not have any cats or dogs already, as long as the

kitten can be confined indoors until it is old enough for its first shots. If this is not practicable, it should stay with its mother until twelve weeks old.

◆ PEDIGREE KITTENS ◆

Pedigree cats are expensive, and not without reason. The cost of buying a pedigree female cat of suitable quality and the cost of the stud fee are only the first of many expenses (*see 'Breeding From Your Cat'*).

There are more than one hundred breeds to choose from, including the different coat colours and patterns within each breed. If you do not have a firm idea about the breed you would like, look

BELOW

It is not just rescued 'moggies' that are looking for homes; most cat breed clubs will have adult cats of your chosen breed needing homes too.

◉ RESCUE CENTRES ◉

There are so many unwanted cats in need of good homes that it makes sense to take one from a rescue centre. It is not just moggies that are looking for homes. In the UK, all breed clubs affiliated to the Governing Council of the Cat Fancy (GCCF) have an appointed welfare officer in charge of rehoming, so if a particular pedigree breed is your preference, contact the club for that breed. No such equivalent is available in the USA, although a club will probably be able to advise you. If you decide to adopt a rescue, be prepared to go through the third degree by way of interrogation. No responsible rehoming service will allow a cat to leave the premises unless the officer is absolutely sure that the cat is going to have a home for the rest of its life and will not become a rehomer again in a few weeks' time. It may seem as if you are being interviewed as stringently as if you were adopting a baby. The officer may even make a visit to your home to ensure it is suitable, and follow up in a few weeks' time to check that the cat has settled well with the family.

All rescue work relies on charitable donation, so be prepared to put your hand in your pocket. Any cat taken as a rescue will have been thoroughly checked over by a veterinarian, have been neutered, and have received the necessary inoculations. This all costs money. A good permanent home for the cat is the main priority, but if you are able to afford a donation, do so.

Rescue centres often have a multitude of pretty, healthy cats ready for adoption (ABOVE). This beautiful, albeit one-eyed, cat (LEFT) started life with a deprived kittenhood. Neglected and unwanted, she succumbed to cat flu, causing ulceration to one eye which had to be removed. Months on, with much loving care and the correct veterinary treatment, she is a cat that her new owner is justifiably proud of.

CHOOSING A CAT

LEFT
A visit to a cat show will provide the opportunity to see many different breeds and to meet the owners and breeders; most are very helpful and will outline the finer points of their particular breed to aid you with your decision.

through some cat-breed guides in the library. Each breed is intrinsically different, not just in appearance, but in character, too. Even within the breeds, some colour variations have slightly different temperaments. Having read about all the different varieties – and do remember that not all breeds of cat are available in every country – the next thing to do is meet up with the cats 'in the fur'. A visit to an all-breed cat show will give you the opportunity to see as many breeds as possible.

At the show, you will probably decide on the breed that most suits you. In the USA, you can buy cats direct from a show. In the UK, however, cat shows are only a shop window; you are not allowed to actually buy. But you will probably meet breeders of the types of cat that interest you. If not, you may know someone with a cat of the same breed, who can advise you of a reputable breeder. If this is not possible, contact the appropriate breed club, which will run a list of kittens available and so should be able to put you in contact with a local breeder

(the appropriate governing body can provide you with this information). Specialist cat magazines carry advertisements of pedigree kittens for sale, as do local newspapers. Bear in mind that some breeds are rarer than others, and so you may have to wait several months for a kitten and even travel some distance to see the litter. Remember that cats at shows will not always act as they do at home, so it is very important to visit a breeder to see what the character of your preferred breed is like in a domestic environment before making a firm decision.

Arrange to visit only one cattery in a day, as it is easy to carry infections from one household of kittens to another. When you first contact the breeder, telephone for an appointment. You will probably be asked many questions at this point, but only to reassure both yourself and the breeder that you are not going to be wasting each other's time. Cat breeding is essentially a hobby, not a business; most breeders have a home, family and job to cope with as well as their cats and so are busier than most of us.

It is a politeness to let the breeder know just how many of you will be arriving on the appointed day, and if for any reason you are delayed, or unable to keep the appointment, telephone to say so. Try not to treat the occasion as a visit to the zoo and bring the whole family along – you are visiting a stranger's home. For the first visit, you and your partner are quite enough; leave any children behind. Never outstay your welcome, and although there will be many questions to be asked, try to keep them to

BELOW

When visiting a breeder, it is usual to be able to see the mother cat with her kittens. However, you may not be invited to handle very young kittens that have not been inoculated and are vulnerable to infection.

RIGHT

These kittens have been brought up in the breeder's home and are used to all the usual household accoutrements. If raised in an outside cattery, a young kitten may take considerable time to settle into a domestic environment.

a minimum. If you are serious about buying a kitten, there will be plenty of opportunity to ask advice later. Realize that no reputable breeder would allow a kitten to go to a new home on the very first visit – this will be one of several more to come.

If, at this first meeting, there are kittens in the home, do not be put off if you are not allowed to handle them, or are asked to disinfect your hands. This is no reflection on your personal hygiene, but a simple precaution against infection. However, you will be able to assess the general condition of the cats and kittens, and decide if this is going to be the breeder of your choice. You will most likely be asked to think it over for a week before making a final decision. Then, the breeder will invite you back, this time to meet any other members of your family, including children. Some young children are excellent with cats but others, especially those who have never shared their home with a cat before, may treat kittens like toys and be too rough with them. Many small children are especially fascinated by eyes and could easily accidentally poke a kitten's eye and damage it.

If children are too boisterous, do not be offended if the breeder refuses to sell you a kitten; wait a year or two until the children are old enough to realize that each cat is a living creature with its own personality, and so needs to be treated with the respect it deserves.

If all goes well, you will probably be asked for a deposit against the cost of the kitten. This works both ways: you are now assured that your kitten is definitely booked for you, and the breeder knows that your intentions are honourable. Deposits are returnable for good reasons such as illness or change of circumstance, but if you change your mind on a whim, do not expect to get your money back. The kitten has been reserved for you and if this commitment is not honoured the breeder has the added expense of keeping the kitten for longer, and maybe of readvertising it.

From the beginning, it is important to tell the breeder the reason for buying a kitten: is it purely as a pet, or do you wish to show or maybe even breed from it? No breeder would wish to see an example of their breeding exhibited on the show bench if it is not up to standard, as it

would reflect on them and their breeding programme. In the UK, it is likely that those kittens unsuitable for breeding will have been placed on the non-active register, as this precludes breeding without the breeders' written consent to the GCCF. In the USA, there is no non-active register, however 'not for breeding' can be noted on the blue slip, or cats can be registered as neuters or spays after the relevant operation.

A pet-quality kitten of your chosen breed will be just the same as one sold for show and breeding, but may have some small fault, such as a tail kink or slightly misaligned jaw that would cause a show judge to withhold a prize. These are traits that you would not want to perpetuate through breeding.

All kittens have cost the same amount to raise, so many breeders will charge the same for pet-quality kittens as they do for those designated for the show bench or a breeding programme. Others differentiate, and charge more for show and breeding kittens than pets. At the end of the day, all cats should also be pets and, if you happen to enjoy going to shows, then this is an added bonus – the character and temperament of the cat will be the same regardless of the finer breed requisites laid down in the standard of points.

When you come to collect your kitten it should be at least twelve weeks old, wormed and fully inoculated. Make sure that you bring a sturdy cat carrier with you. It will probably be the first time the kitten has had to travel in a car, bus or

train and this can be a frightening experience, so it will feel much more secure if contained in a carrier.

Before leaving, the breeder should provide you with:
- Inoculation certificate
- Pedigree of at least four generations
- Transfer form
- Diet sheet, outlining the types of food the kitten is used to and times of feeding

. WHAT TO LOOK FOR . IN A KITTEN

Whatever your preference, pedigree or non-pedigree, the kitten should be fit, healthy, happy and friendly.

The main difference between pedigree and non-pedigree cats is that you know the parentage of pedigrees. To a certain extent, health and temperament can be inherited; if you know who the mother and father are, and have met them, you will have a fair idea of the character your kitten will have when it grows up. All

BELOW
If purchasing a pedigree cat you will have probably visited the kitten at the breeder's home and met its parents. Many characteristics are genetically based, so if your kitten's parents are healthy and sweet-tempered, it is likely their offspring will exhibit the same traits.

ABOVE
When collecting your new kitten from the breeder, do ensure that you take a safe cat carrier with you so the kitten feels secure during the journey to its new home.

1 The ears should be clean and free from parasites.

2 The eyes should be clear and bright, without any trace of debris in the corners.

3 The mouth and gums should have a healthy pink tinge.

4 For a show specimen, the tail should be straight without any sign of a kink.

5 The coat should be clean and clear of parasites.

6 The anal region should be clean with no trace of faecal matter.

7 The tummy should feel full and soft; any hardness in this region could denote the presence of worm infestation.

ABOVE
Be wary of accepting a cat that appears frightened of humans. Unused to domestic home life, it will take a long time to adjust to a new home and will require many patient hours of tender loving care to settle in.

Here are some indications to health and temperament you should look out for:

● Kittens should be used to being handled from birth, and should not be frightened of humans.

● If the kitten hisses or spits at you, or seems timid and nervous, you are better off looking elsewhere for your pet.

● The kittens should all have bright eyes and clean coats with no sign of parasitic infestation.

● Their tummies should feel plump but soft; any hardness could indicate worm infestation.

● The ears, too, should be clean; any brown, waxy deposits may mean the kitten has ear mites.

● Look at the kittens' litter tray: is it clean, too? A strong smell along with runny excrement could indicate some infection.

SETTLING YOUR CAT OR KITTEN INTO ITS NEW HOME

Before you collect your cat or kitten, make sure that you have all the necessary equipment. Do not leave this until the last minute, or you may find the shops shut: washing up bowls and roasting trays prove expensive alternatives to a litter tray, although they serve in an emergency.

The basic items needed to start with are:

● Litter tray
● Cat litter and litter scoop
● Food and water bowls
● Food
● Sleeping basket and bedding
● Cat carrier
● Scratching post and toys
● Collar and tag

kittens should be used to the usual household hubbub: the sounds of dishwashers, washing machines, vacuum cleaners and television sets should not frighten them.

Be wary of buying a kitten that has been brought up outside in a cattery, as it may take a long time to settle into the alien environment of a normal home. Try to get your kitten from a similar family situation to your own; for example, if you already have a dog, find a kitten that has been brought up with dogs and is used to them. The same goes for households with children and babies. It is traumatic enough for a kitten to be moved to a different home, without having strange new creatures to contend with too.

The best time to introduce a cat into your home is when you have plenty of time to spare, and there are few other people
Continued page 41

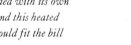
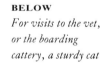

ABOVE
Separate food and
water bowls are a
must; the plastic
variety is probably the
most useful.

ABOVE
A litter tray will be
needed if the cat is not
allowed outside;
covered trays prevent
cat litter being
scattered over the
floor.

ABOVE
A collar is essential if
the cat is to be allowed
outdoors.

ABOVE
A cat should be
provided with its own
bed, and this heated
one would fit the bill
nicely.

BELOW
For visits to the vet,
or the boarding
cattery, a sturdy cat
carrier will be needed.

RIGHT
A cat scratching post
will save the furniture
untold damage; this
one incorporates a
swinging ball for extra
play value.

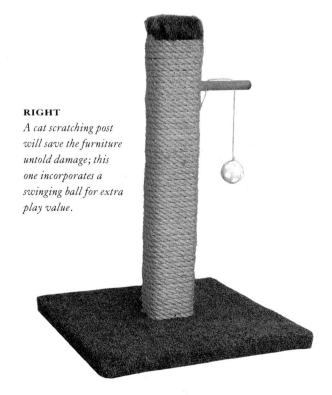

KITTENS AND PLAY

ABOVE
A 'spider' toy made of a ball of wool and pipe cleaners is being cautiously inspected. A tug on the string, causing the toy to move, will probably incite the predatory instincts of a kitten. A toy such as this should only be offered for play under strict supervision as the pipe cleaners contain wire which, if chewed, might harm a kitten.

Kittens love to play and this provides much more than just simple pleasure to a young developing cat. Play involves the use of all the muscles in the body, and aids strong, healthy growth and development. Two kittens will happily play together and this encourages social development too; they will also enjoy the added stimulus of toys to play with. A sole kitten actually *needs* toys if it is to develop, both socially and physically, into a healthy, well-adjusted adult.

A play pole, covered in rope or similar fabric, will encourage the kitten to scratch. This saves both your carpets and furnishings, and provides a most necessary function; the kitten will both clean and sharpen its claws while scratching. This action exercises not only the claws and paws, but also extends to the muscles

in the legs and the back, and so is of great importance to the cat's general wellbeing. Moreover, this is why any owner should think twice about de-clawing, a deplorable operation that, fortunately, is prohibited in the UK.

Toys, especially those scented with cat mint, will also cause great excitement and interest, and ensures that the olfactory lobes are exercised too. In addition, they will stimulate a kitten confined to a domestic environment to simulate the natural responses it would have when catching prey. Noisy toys will cause interest, too, whether they be by way of a squeak or a rattle! This all helps to keep the ear senses well tuned.

Just as with a small child, toys provide much, much more than mere fun – they are part of the process of not just learning, but also of growing up.

BELOW
A play pole with toys suspended from it will encourage a young cat to play, exercise and scratch – activities vital to a cat's wellbeing.

TOP AND ABOVE
Kittens, like children, often discover a play value in toys other than those intended. This toy incorporates a catnip-scented ball and is designed to encourage the kitten to pat it back and forth on its flexible stalk. This contrary kitten, however, is determined to wrestle the stalk from its fixing.

RIGHT
If you have chosen an adult cat, you will need to give it a lot of time and attention to help it settle into a new domestic environment.

BELOW
Cats and children can make ideal sleeping companions. But remember, this will be a hard habit to break and the cat will expect to sleep in the bed for the rest of its life.

around. Most kittens settle in quickly but it may take a little while to introduce an adult cat to new surroundings. If you are at work during the day, try to take a few days off either side of the weekend so that you and your new cat have some time to spend together. If you have children, it may be better to get the kitten accustomed to your home while they are at school.

Before the cat arrives, decide the most suitable sites for the litter tray and feeding bowls. Let the cat see these as soon as it arrives – it may need the litter tray immediately; accidents will happen and the stress of travelling from one home to another can play havoc on the bowels!

Also, think about the cat's sleeping arrangements. Cats like to sleep in the warmest part of the house, and they like company too, so given the choice your new cat will opt to sleep in bed with you. Old habits die hard; you may be tempted to allow your kitten to sleep with you for the first night or two, but it will be hard to persuade it a few weeks later that these

BELOW
Cat beds come in many shapes and sizes and many cats find an 'igloo' most acceptable. Site the bed in a fairly warm room.

ABOVE
Make sure that you site the litter tray in a place convenient for both your cat and family and leave it there. The cat will become understandably confused if the tray is moved to a different location in the house.

some rooms cat-free, so make this clear from the beginning by keeping the doors closed. Once a cat has been inside a room, and later finds the door locked, it will be forever miaowing to get back in, or scratching at the carpet.

The main place your cat or kitten will inhabit is the living room as this is the area most used by you and your family, so let this be its first room to explore. Remember that your home is alien territory to a kitten and it may be quite frightened by suddenly being exposed to a large house with lots of rooms. Introducing an adult cat, neutered or not, to new surroundings may well evoke territorial behaviour such as spraying, which can be difficult to cure.

Whether you have opted for an adult cat or a kitten, introduce it to your home room by room over a period of several days. As the cat becomes more confident of the layout of the house, it can be left to wander freely indoors.

Do be careful to keep the cat inside for at least a week, even if eventually you are going to allow it free access to your garden. Cats are great escapologists, so keep the front and back doors shut, and make sure that the windows are closed too. It is surprising how small a gap a cat can crawl through and, if it does get out, it may panic in new surroundings and get lost or, worse still, run over.

ABOVE

Cats are natural escape artists, and if they know something interesting lies on the other side of a door, they will make every attempt to get out.

are not its designated sleeping quarters, and you may find yourself with a furry sleeping partner for life. If you do not want to share your bed with your cat, make this quite clear from the outset. Make a cosy nest for your kitten in its own basket; put in suitable bedding materials, a hot water bottle and some toys; place the basket in a warm spot in the room you feel is best for the cat's night-time accommodation – and keep your bedroom door shut.

Cats do not like unnecessary upheaval. When they know exactly where they can find their food, litter tray and bed, stay with this arrangement. Never lock the cat out of the room that contains the litter tray, or you may find a mess to clear up in the morning.

Gradually introduce your cat to those areas of your home that you are going to give it access to. You may prefer to keep

INTRODUCING YOUR CAT • TO OTHER ANIMALS • IN THE HOME

Your new cat or kitten will probably be the centre of attention when you first bring it home, but do not exclude any existing pets from your attentions as this will make them very jealous of the new intruder and may prolong the settling process. Make sure that both animals get the same amount of attention.

If you already own an adult cat and want to introduce another, it can take

RIGHT
*Finding the door
firmly shut, this cat
has jumped onto a
suitable work surface
and, undaunted, starts
to paw at the bolt.*

LEFT
*Having achieved its
purpose, the cat is now
free to explore the
great wide yonder. If
you want to prohibit
your cat from
roaming, outside or
within the house, keep
all doors and windows
firmly shut.*

CHOOSING A CAT

CATS AND CHILDREN

If you have children, explain to them that the new cat is not a furry toy. Children are usually good with animals, but some can be a little over-enthusiastic and excited. Teach children the correct way to hold a cat; explain that tails are not designed to be pulled and that the creature should be treated with respect. Your children will love to play with the kitten, but make sure that they do not get too rough with it; young bones are delicate and can easily be broken. Remember, too, that cats have a very good self-defence system; if your child gets too rumbustious, the cat will quite likely use its claws and there

A single cat and an only child (BELOW) can be devoted companions.

will be tears before bedtime. To prevent eye injuries, teach children not to push their faces up close to the cat. This is also the time to teach children to adopt the sensible hygiene practice of washing hands after handling animals, particularly before meals, and always after carrying out of litter tray duties.

Most of all this is common sense. Take plenty of time with your new cat, introducing it gradually to its new home, and you should find that you have a happy, contented and sociable pet for many years to come.

Children should be taught the correct way to handle a cat and this little girl (ABOVE) has got it all right.

Cats love to be part of the family but a brief instruction from mother to a young child will ensure that they all live in harmony (RIGHT).

BELOW
An established pet and a cat new to the household can, with sensitive handling, become the best of friends as this huge, solid ginger-and-white moggie boy and elegant, slender Siamese girl demonstrate.

LEFT
Cats that have been brought up together since kittenhood invariably get on well together, even if not of the same litter.

quite a time to get them to settle down together. The resident cat will not appreciate the newcomer at first and, if you are not careful, there will be a lot of caterwauling and fur flying. Introductions must be done gradually.

Smell is very important to cats, so take a blanket or piece of fabric from your home and put it in the carrier you collect your new cat in. It will smell, not only of your house, but of the resident animals, and will give the cat a chance to sniff out the family before it gets home. It helps if the newcomer smells familiar too, so if you use perfume or cologne, rub a little on the new cat before you bring it into your home, and it will seem less of a threat to the resident feline. You could also try putting sardine or pilchard juice on each cat, which may seem strange, but the most important thing is for the cats to smell the same, and this idea might even get them to start washing each other.

Food is another good way to get cats to accept each other; feed them in the same room, from separate bowls. As the cats become engrossed in their meal, gradually move the bowls nearer together. When the meals are finished, the cats will invariably start to wash; the nearer together they are, the more likely they are to indulge in social grooming, a sure sign of feline acceptance.

When you sit down for the evening, make sure that each cat has a vacant lap on which to sit. If you live on your own, get a friend to drop by for a while. This ensures that both cats feel they are getting

ABOVE
A kitten pen is designed to keep small kittens away from harm. It can also be used to keep one cat away from another during the initial settling-in period.

the same amount of attention. Swap cats from time to time; in this way they will pick up each other's smells and be assured that the other cat is not a threat. Use similar tactics when introducing them to different rooms; one cat in one room, one in the other, and swap over after an hour or so. This gives each time to sniff out the opposition.

If you have a kitten pen, use it during this settling-in period. With one cat in the pen, and the other free to wander around the room, they will be able to look at each other, but if they do decide to have a confrontation, will not actually get close enough to cause harm.

It is much easier to settle a kitten with an adult than it is to introduce two grown-up cats. Most adult cats, even males, will show a kind of parental instinct to a small newcomer. All the above procedures apply to introducing a kitten, but it should take much less time for the two to accept each other.

❦ HOW TO HOLD A CAT ❦

A cat should always be held in such a way that it feels secure. Gently cradle the back and rear quarters with one hand and support the shoulders with the other so the cat feels reassured that it is in safe hands.

Introducing your cat or kitten to the family dog should be treated with caution. If the kitten has grown up with a dog, and your dog is used to cats, there should be few problems. If not, tread very carefully. Some breeds of dog, such as many of the terrier varieties, are instinctive 'ratters' and may react to a kitten as they would to a rabbit. Again, if you have one, use a kitten pen so that the dog and cat can see and smell each other without the risk of either being hurt. If there is a fight, it is quite likely that the dog will come off worse: cats are extremely agile, move quickly, can jump and have sharp claws.

Whichever animals you are introducing – cats, kittens or dogs – it is *most important* that they are not left unsupervised until you are completely satisfied that they have integrated. In the meantime, put them in separate rooms and shut the doors firmly whenever you have to leave the house.

ABOVE AND RIGHT
Introducing a strange dog and cat to each other should only be done under supervision. Despite the difference in size it is more likely that the dog will come off the worse for wear. After an initial sniff these two were soon on hugging terms.

CARING FOR YOUR CAT

When you first bring your new cat or kitten home it should already have been inoculated, wormed and checked over by a veterinary surgeon for general health. Now it is your duty to keep the cat fit and healthy; routine maintenance, and a balanced diet, are the basis of this.

CHOOSING A VETERINARY SURGEON

The first priority is to find a veterinary surgeon, and to register with the practice. Do not wait until your cat is ill, or has had some accident; you never know when your cat might need medical attention, and if you and your cat are already known to a vet, he or she will have all the background information.

Although all vets are GPs, and have a broad knowledge of all animals, some practices are specifically for domestic pets. These are found mainly in large towns and cities, where most of the patients are cats and dogs. In the country, especially in farming communities, most vets will be more used to dealing with large animals, such as sheep and cattle. It is important to find a vet who has a good knowledge of cats, and is up to date on the various illnesses and ailments that can affect the feline, along with their appropriate treatment. Some years ago, a cat breeder friend of mine moved from a city environment to a remote country area. When she approached the local vet to have a litter of kittens inoculated, he shook his head in bewilderment. He was used to servicing the local farming community, who thought of cats as mousers, and would not dream of spending their hard-earned money on inoculating them. Having never been asked for such a service before, he did not carry any

vaccine in stock; it took over a week to order it and cost considerably more than my friend was used to paying.

Nonetheless, it is useful to find a vet locally; it is pointless to register with the best cat practice in the country if it is going to take several hours to travel there. If you have bought your kitten from a local breeder, or obtained a cat from a local rescue centre, ask them to recommend a vet. Ask local cat owners, too, which practice they go to. Some of the larger cat clubs have local advisers who may be able to help you. Personal recommendation is always best, but if this fails, look through the commercial pages of the phone book; this will list all the veterinary practices.

When you have selected a veterinary surgeon, telephone the practice and make an appointment to meet. Ask if the vet would like to meet your cat too; after all this is who will be the patient. It is important for you to feel confident in your vet's abilities and approach. If all seems well, and the three of you get along together, register the cat there. Make sure that you take the inoculation certificate with you, as the vet will need to log this information in order to remind you when the annual booster shot is due.

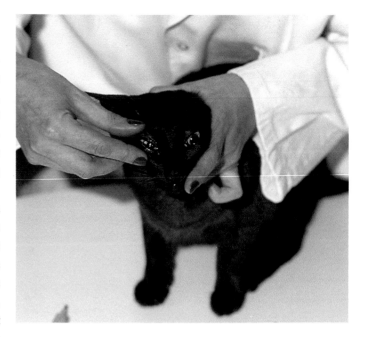

ABOVE
Cat owners should register their feline charges with a local veterinary practice as soon as possible, and not just when treatment is needed. Even with minor ailments it is important to visit the vet for a correct diagnosis, a prescription, if necessary, and advice for the correct administration of any medication, such as eye ointment. Never apply or administer any kind of medicinal preparation developed for human use.

BELOW
When the annual booster inoculation is due, ask the vet to give your cat a thorough health check at the same time.

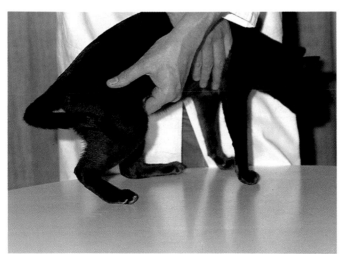

ROUTINE CARE

A part from supplying your cat with a balanced diet (*see 'Feeding Your Cat'*) there are other little things you can do to help it stay fit and healthy.

Regular grooming (*see 'Grooming Your Cat'*) will help keep the cat's coat sparkling and free of tangles, and will help to stop fur balls forming. You will also be able to spot any sign of fleas, or other external parasites, and treat them before they become a problem. In the same way, you will see any telltale signs of tapeworm infestation (*see 'Parasites'*).

Claws, eyes, ears and teeth all benefit from regular examination. Try to make this a regular routine, perhaps every fortnight or so. Once the cat is accustomed to the idea, it will probably start to enjoy these little sessions.

• CLAWS •

C lipping your cat's claws will save your furniture and, possibly yourself, from damage. Cats that go outside will naturally strop tree trunks to keep their claws to a manageable length. Pro-

LEFT
If a cat is allowed outside it will use tree trunks or wooden posts for stropping, thereby preventing its claws from growing too long.

LEFT
A cat scratching post, with playthings attached, will give your cat hours of pleasure with the added bonus of saving the furniture and carpets from its sharp claws.

viding a scratching post in your home will satisfy an indoor cat's need to scratch to a certain extent. A word of warning: never cover the scratching post with the same carpet as that which furnishes your home; this may look aesthetically pleasing, but will confuse the cat, who will think the carpet is an extension of the post, and will scratch that too.

Clipping claws should be done with care, and it is best to get your vet to show you how to do this the first time. Holding the cat firmly (you may need a friend to help), push the paw pad of each individual claw inward, one at a time; this will reveal the unsheathed claw. You will now see two quite different colours to the claw, a pink area in the middle, surrounded by a whitish covering culminating in the pointed end of the claw. The pink area contains the blood supply and the nerves and, if cut, would cause pain and bleeding. The sharp, white point of the claw is composed only of dead cells, and is perfectly safe to cut. Special claw clippers can be bought from the pet store, but ordinary nail clippers designed for humans are just as effective, and a lot cheaper. Your cat may object to claw cutting at first but, once introduced to the routine, it will soon accept a fortnightly clipping session.

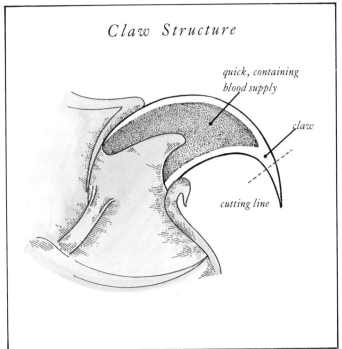

Claw Structure

quick, containing
blood supply

claw

cutting line

*If your cat is to be
confined indoors
without access to trees
where it could
naturally strop its
claws, it is a wise
precaution to blunt the
tips of the claws to
remove the sharp
point. This can be done
with ordinary toenail
clippers (**ABOVE**) or
with specialized feline
claw clippers
(**RIGHT**). See the
diagram (**ABOVE
RIGHT**) before
attempting to do this;
ascertaining the
correct cutting line is
vitally important to
prevent injury.*

BELOW
*Any 'sleep' left
deposited in the corner
of the eye can be
removed gently with a
piece of moistened
cotton wool.*

◆ EYES ◆

It is not unusual to find small deposits of matter in the corner of the eye; this can be removed with some cotton wool moistened with cooled boiled water or, if you are careful, with your clean little finger – but be careful not to poke the cat in the eye. The third eyelid (haw or nictitating membrane) should not be visible in a healthy cat.

The cat is unusual in that it has three eyelids, two of which move up and down like our own. The haw moves across the eye from the side nearest the nose towards the outer edge. If dust, or even cat litter, gets in your cat's eye, it will cause the haw to come up – if this is the case, bathing the eye in a little dilute eye wash will have a soothing effect. However, a visible haw can be an early warning of impending illness and, if it is still up after twenty-

four hours, you should consult the vet. A rough guideline: if only one haw is up the chances are that there is a foreign body in the eye, but if both are up it is likely that the cat is unwell.

If the cat seems to have runny eyes, especially if accompanied by sneezing, it may be sickening for cat flu. Or it could be suffering an allergic reaction.

ABOVE

Ears can be cleaned with either moistened cotton wool or, with care, a cotton bud but be sure never to delve too deep into the ear canal.

• EARS •

The ears should smell and look clean, with no sign of waxy build-up. The pinna, or exterior ear, can be cleaned with a little moistened cotton wool or, very carefully, with a cotton bud. Never delve deep into the ear canal, as this could cause damage. Any brown, waxy debris may indicate ear mite infestation and, if this is suspected, it should be diagnosed and treated by your vet.

• TEETH •

The teeth should look clean, and the breath smell sweet. Diet (*see 'Feeding Your Cat'*) is very important for the development of healthy teeth in early years. In order to keep gums healthy, and to prevent the build-up of tartar and plaque, your cat should always be given something to chew on such as a non-splintering bone, dried meat or certain suitable dried biscuits. If your cat persistently scratches at its face, or refuses to eat, it may have a loose tooth, gingivitis (gum inflammation) or both. Contact the vet immediately as an extraction and treatment may be needed.

• OTHER POINTS • TO CHECK

Always look out for any unusual lump or bump. This may be a simple sebaceous cyst; it could also be the start of a tumour. Any change in temperament could indicate injury or illness.

It cannot be stressed enough how important regular observation and examination of your cat is. Remember that your vet will usually only see your cat once a year for the annual check-up and boosters. You know your cat best as it lives with you twenty-four hours a day and so you are the person who will notice if the cat is 'not quite right'. Do not be afraid to mention the smallest change in your cat's shape, size, personality or behaviour to your vet; what may seem trivial to you could be vital information that will help provide a correct diagnosis.

ABOVE

Regular examination of your cat's mouth will give you an indication of any impending problems. Look out for inflamed gums or loose teeth and if this is the case contact your vet immediately.

FEEDING YOUR CAT

A proper, well-balanced diet is of paramount importance to the health and wellbeing of your cat. Food is not just a fuel to keep the body ticking over; it directly affects the condition of your cat's teeth and bones, all the internal organs, especially the bowels, and ultimately the chosen diet will be reflected in the condition of the cat's coat.

No matter where you have acquired your cat, it should be in the peak of condition when you accept it into your home. If you bought a kitten from a breeder, you should have been given a diet sheet to help it through the first few months. Cat or kitten, you have taken on responsibility for its welfare, and nothing is more important than correct feeding.

Cats are creatures of habit and so it is important, right from the start, to implement a regime for feeding times and the location of food and water bowls. The diet that the cat requires will vary according to its age. A kitten needs feeding little and often, and the same applies to an older cat. A healthy adult cat needs fewer

but larger meals. An invalid cat may require a special diet and your vet will advise you on this.

EQUIPMENT AND WHERE TO PUT IT

M ost owners find that the kitchen is the most convenient place to feed their cat, as this is where food is stored and prepared. It is probably not a good

ABOVE
To avoid forever tripping over food and water bowls, consider feeding your cat on a free work surface in the kitchen.

BELOW
Feeding bowls: (from left to right) time-controlled, glass, metal, earthenware, plastic, double-bowl. There are advantages, and some disadvantages, with each of these types. Select bowls that work for you and are acceptable to your cat.

ABOVE

Product cat food: (clockwise from 11 o'clock) dried biscuits, semi-moist 'nuggets', canned food, vacuum-sealed punnet, dried protein diet. All these foods provide nutrition, but for a well-balanced and pleasing diet offer your cat a selection of these prepared foods and fresh food.

idea to feed the cat on the floor, as you will be forever tripping over the bowls. A tray containing the food and water bowls placed on a spare work surface keeps everything in one place and out of the way. If you have a utility room, this may be more convenient. Once established, keep to the routine; your cat needs to have permanent access to fresh water and so needs to know where to find the water bowl.

Bowls

There are many different kinds of food bowl available, some better and more practical than others.

PLASTIC bowls are probably the most common as they are durable, almost un-breakable and easy to clean. Not all are dishwasher-proof.

METAL bowls are indestructible and can be sterilized at a high temperature without damage.

EARTHENWARE bowls are solid and will not tip over easily but are easily broken or chipped if dropped.

GLASS bowls are not a good idea; they may look pretty, but if dropped they will break with the risk that fragments of

glass will get embedded in the cat's paws or, worse still, be swallowed.

DOUBLE BOWLS which can hold both food and water look like a good idea; however, if the water needs changing before the cat has finished all the food, it is almost impossible to empty the water without spilling the food.

TIME-CONTROLLED feeding bowls can be a boon to anyone who is out at work all day. These consist of two removable bowls inside a lidded container with a programmable timer. You set the time that the cat should be fed, and the lid pops up to allow the cat to get to its food. In hot countries, this has the added bonus that it keeps flies off the food. One drawback: some cats do not take long to realize how the time control works!

• CHOICE OF FOOD •

Cats are natural carnivores and a look at their teeth will confirm this: large canines to tear flesh; tiny incisors as the cat has little need to nibble at grass and vegetation; and a hefty set of molars to aid chewing. In the wild, a cat catches prey and eats it whole: feathers, fur, bones and, quite importantly, the content of the stomach and bowels; this last item is

ABOVE
Some breeds of cat have a greater predilection to obesity than others. British Shorthairs fall into this category and their diet should be carefully monitored, especially if the cat is a less active neuter.

usually vegetable matter which provides trace elements the cat would not otherwise have access to.

In modern society, we tend to frown on cats catching birds and mice; it is a messy business and opening a tin or packet seems a more hygienic way to provide the cat with its basic dietary needs. The key to providing a good diet is balance, so consider all the different varieties available.

There are so many kinds of cat food on the market that both you and your cat will be spoiled for choice. Variety is the spice of life; by feeding your cat a combination of some of the different foods available, you will ensure an interesting, balanced and adequate diet.

CANNED FOOD is probably the most popular. It is convenient, easy to store, and should contain a perfect balance of nutrients, vitamins and minerals essential for a cat's wellbeing. Some brands have a special kitten formula, especially designed for the dietary needs of a younger cat. Canned foods are available in many different flavours, so your cat will always have variety. One reservation – some cats find that certain brands of canned food are too rich and can cause diarrhoea.

BISCUITS provide an interesting and crunchy supplement to your cat's diet, but should never be used as the sole food supply. A few sprinkled on your cat's usual food will provide exercise for the jaws and help keep the teeth and gums healthy.

DRIED PROTEIN diets are a recent development. They are based on scientific principles and are usually formulated from hydrolysed beef protein. They are the ultimate complete balanced diet, and contain every possible vitamin, mineral and trace element a cat needs. They are easy to store, convenient to serve, and have the bonus that they can be left down when you are out and will not spoil like canned food. There are special kinds available, such as formulas for kittens and 'less active' cats.

SEMI-MOIST 'NUGGETS' in vacuum-sealed pouches are a food many cats find irresistible. They are easy to store and, once opened, do not deteriorate as fast as the canned varieties. They make an excellent 'treat' for your cat, but should not form the main constituent of its diet.

VACUUM-SEALED PUNNETS are another new kind of food containing fresh-cooked fish, meat or chicken. These contain no preservatives or colouring and so are especially suitable for cats with delicate stomachs.

FRESH FOOD should, ideally, be offered for one of the meals each day. It could be cooked, filleted chicken, rabbit or fish, but be sure that all bones are removed, as they could easily get stuck in the throat. Almost all cats enjoy cooked meats such as beef and lamb. Some prefer raw food, and for them, a little raw, lean beef will be greeted with enthusiasm – it is unwise to give your cat raw fish, chicken or other kinds of meat. If you are feeding fresh food, do make sure that you buy 'human consumption' quality; some butchers sell 'pet mince' which is made from fatty beef and, although suitable for dogs, can cause digestive problems in cats.

TABLE SCRAPS are often fed to cats and can provide a valuable extra source of nutrition. Vegetables, especially greens, are particularly useful, as they echo the natural diet of a cat in the wild. Cooked meat bones – not chicken or rabbit – will give the cat something to chew on. Never offer a cat bones that might splinter, but leftovers from the roast joint, or chops, will give the cat hours of pleasure and will also help keep the teeth and gums exercised and healthy.

VITAMIN AND MINERAL SUPPLEMENTS can be bought at most pet stores. Read the instructions on the container thoroughly, as it is possible to overdose your cat on some supplements. If you feel that your cat is lacking some vital mineral or vitamin, consult your vet.

FEEDING: HOW MUCH AND HOW OFTEN

The average adult, neutered cat needs two meals each day. The amount of food needed depends on the size and build of the cat. As a rough guideline, 250 grams (8 oz) of canned cat food per meal (one small can, or half of a large can) is enough. This is roughly equivalent to a 100-gram (3-oz) portion of freshly cooked fish or chicken.

After the first six to nine months, kittens need a similar amount of food to adult cats, but it should spread over four meals a day; the same goes for older 'senior citizen' cats – little and often is the right approach.

Pregnant or lactating queens, and working stud cats, need a different diet with vitamin and mineral supplements (*see 'Breeding From Your Cat'*).

Although obese cats are sometimes seen, they are not very common. Cats are usually sensible about their waistlines, and tend not to overindulge. However, some cats, and some breeds in particular, are prone to becoming overweight. As a conscientious cat owner, you will know if your cat is becoming too fat; if you are in doubt contact your vet for advice. Personally, I feel that it is better for a cat to be slightly plump than verging on the anorexic; if it then suffers a slight illness, and does not feed for a while, it has some substance to fall back on.

ABOVE
Encouraging cats at a young age to chew meat from the bone will help the teeth to become stronger and less likely to decay in old age.

GROOMING YOUR CAT

Cats are fastidious animals, and usually manage to keep their fur coats in pristine order. However, as with most things, a little help from a friend does not go amiss; when several cats live together they will indulge in social grooming, and spend hours washing each other. Usually, they will pay special attention to those awkward places that a single cat cannot easily reach, such as behind the ears and the back of the neck.

This does not mean that a human friend cannot help out too; indeed, with our modern urban environment and centrally heated houses, it is important for all cats to have some extra grooming. Both longhaired and shorthaired cats moult; in the wild this would be confined to the warm summer months when the cat needed to shed some of its heavy, winter overcoat. In a home with a controlled temperature, cats moult a little all year round. When a cat grooms itself, a certain amount of fur is ingested, and this can lead to a build-up of fur balls in the stomach (*see Health Care, Ailments and Illnesses*). Regular grooming will help stop these forming.

Introduce your cat to regular grooming sessions as soon as possible; it is

ABOVE
The mother cat will spend many hours making sure her offspring are immaculately clean.

RIGHT
Social grooming is an important aspect of a cat's life – what better than a friend to help wash those inaccessible parts, such as behind the ears.

always easier to get a young animal used to the routine than it is an older animal. From the cat's point of view, once it is used to them, these grooming sessions are thoroughly enjoyable: most cats love being stroked and touched, and a good brushing, combined with some hand grooming, can result in a feline drooling with pleasure.

·GROOMING EQUIPMENT·

When buying any grooming equipment, make sure that you buy from a reputable pet store. The cheapest equipment might seem like a bargain, but is not always the best. It probably will not last as long as a better-quality product and might even damage your cat. Ensure that any metal combs have *blunt*, *rounded* teeth, and that there are no sharp points.

The equipment you need depends on the length of the cat's coat. These are some of the most readily available:

For a shorthaired cat: chamois leather, bristle brush or baby brush, rubber grooming pad, flea comb, bay rum.
For a longhaired cat: wire and bristle double-sided brush, toothbrush, slicker brush, talcum powder, metal comb with alternate long/short teeth, wide-toothed comb.

STEP-BY-STEP TO GROOMING A SHORTHAIR CAT

Shorthairs, on the whole, do not need a tremendous amount of grooming, but still benefit from a regular brush and comb to help remove dead or loose hairs. A polish with chamois leather will also impart a glossy sheen. Some pedigree breeds, such as British Shorthairs and Manx, have particularly thick coats and so special attention needs to be paid to any early signs of a mat forming.

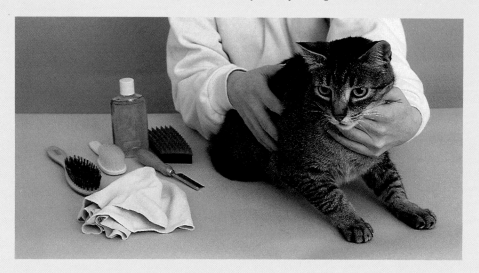

1 For a shorthair cat you will need: (clockwise from top) bay rum, rubber grooming pad, flea comb, chamois leather, bristle or baby brush.

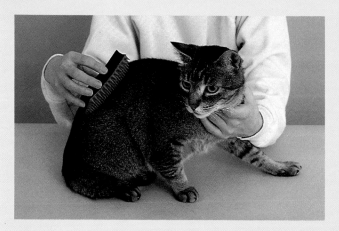

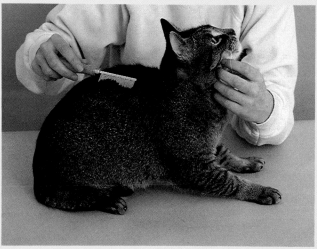

2 A special rubber pad is used to loosen up any dead hairs. The studded surface collects most of the excess fur and provides the added benefit of giving the cat a pleasant massage to stimulate the circulation. It is important not to overdo this first stage as the pad is extremely effective and an over-enthusiastic owner can loosen too much fur. These pads are available in most good pet stores but if it is difficult to find one, try using damp hands as a substitute.

3 Use a fine-toothed comb (usually called a flea comb, but not necessarily used for removing fleas) to comb the coat gently in the opposite direction to that in which it naturally lies; this ensures that the deep-lying dead fur is removed. Then comb thoroughly in the usual way to collect up any remaining debris.

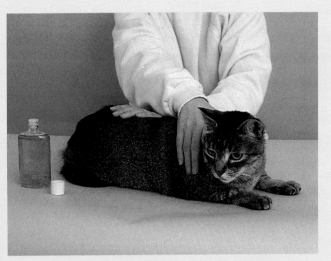

5 Now sprinkle a little bay rum lotion on the hands and, working down the cat from neck to base of tail, gently massage it into the cat's coat. This is effective on any dark-furred, tabby or dark tortie cats as it brings out the brilliance of the colours and leaves a beautiful sheen on the coat. It should not be used on light-coloured cats, as it can cause staining.

4 Use a bristle or baby brush briskly at this point. This will remove any remaining loose fur without disturbing the work already done and causing more hair to shed.

6 Finally, for a really superb finish, treat your cat to a polish with a chamois leather or a piece of silk. Always smooth the fur in the direction that it naturally lies.

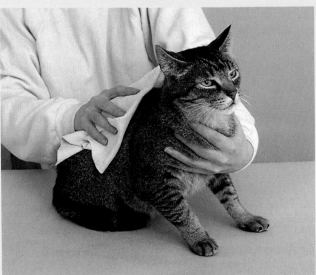

7 A well-groomed cat will look sleek, with a glossy sheen to the coat.

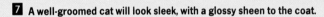

STEP-BY-STEP TO GROOMING A LONGHAIR CAT

Longhaired cats require regular grooming if their coats are to remain free-flowing and tangle-free. Particular attention should be paid to the underparts, especially the belly and trousers, as these are where mats and knots are most likely to occur. Matting is a little like rust on a car – once started, it *tends to spread like wildfire. Regular grooming for at least fifteen minutes each evening will prevent them forming; the alternative is a regular trip to the vet for anaesthetics to be administered and the matted areas surgically removed which is unpleasant for the cat and expensive.*

1 For a longhair cat you will need: (from left to right) wide-toothed comb, toothbrush, wire and bristle double-sided brush, talcum powder, metal comb with long and short teeth, slicker brush.

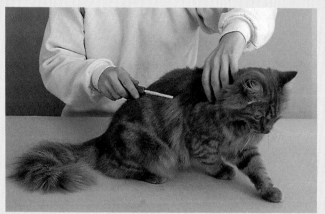

2 Use a wide-toothed comb, or even better one with alternate long and short teeth, to comb gently through the coat in the opposite direction to that in which it usually lies. It may be necessary actually to make partings in the coat and comb it in sections. It is important to make sure that you comb right through to the undercoat to free any knots and tangles, and to comb *gently* through the underparts (this is a delicate part of a cat's anatomy).

3 Lightly sprinkle the coat with baby, or any unperfumed, talcum powder; this helps to ease the brush through the fur, separating each individual hair and adding bulk to the coat. Avoid heavily perfumed 'designer' talcs which can cause an allergic reaction, particularly to the eyes.

4 Brush the coat well, carefully using the wire side of the brush. Be gentle as, although the wire brush is effective, it can cause the delicate hair to break off if used too firmly. If in doubt, omit the wire brushing until you are confident of the way to do it.

5 Now use the bristle side of the brush.

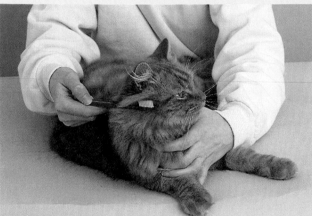

6 Use a toothbrush to brush the facial area. (Most brushes are far too large for this delicate area, but an ordinary toothbrush fits the bill nicely.)

7 A 'slicker' brush, although not essential, can be used for the final stage. This is mainly for the tail and back and will give that finishing touch by fluffing up the fur.

8 The finished result; smooth and tangle-free.

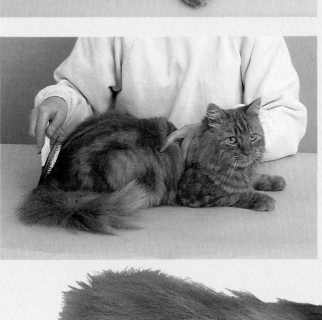

CARING FOR AN ELDERLY CAT

It is impossible to define 'elderly' in terms of years. Cats, like humans, can grow old at any age – some could be classified as elderly at eight years of age, while some still behave like kittens well into their teens. Cats, of course, do not show their age as humans do because they have furry faces, and you cannot see the lines and wrinkles.

Routine maintenance is probably the best way to prevent your cat from becoming prematurely elderly, and this should have begun from kittenhood. However, as a cat grows older, so do all its internal organs; they have served the cat for many years and are bound to start degenerating at some point. Some cats will suffer from heart problems, liver or kidney failure; others may become prone to arthritis and rheumatic problems. Some live to a ripe old age without suffering from any of these. If the cat has been well cared for all its life, then you have done all you can to minimize the chance of your cat becoming frail in old age. Remember also, that some weaknesses can be inherited and there is little you can do about that.

In general, treat your senior cat with the sort of care and respect you would a favourite grandmother. Plenty of love and attention is a priority and can work wonders; regular, balanced meals that are neither too rich nor too bland and contain a good balance of roughage will ensure that the cat is getting the essential nutrients and enough fibre for the bowels to work well; a controlled, warm environment will help to fend off chills and chest complaints; exercise will help to keep the joints mobile and the muscles toned – playing the occasional game will probably be greatly appreciated.

Watch your cat for any change in behaviour which could indicate that some vital organ is not functioning correctly; if the problem is diagnosed before degeneration has gone too far, it will be possible to keep your cat alive for a considerable time with the correct medication. The diagnosis must be carried out by your veterinary surgeon, who will probably take a series of blood, urine and stool samples to isolate the problem. Your job is to observe and let the vet know how exactly the cat is behaving differently.

ABOVE
Elderly cats often suffer from dental problems such as gum disease and loose teeth. Teeth may have to be extracted, but this will not prevent your cat from eating the foods it is used to.

Look out for the following indications of ill health:

● An apparent lack of appetite may be caused by pain from dental problems, a common complaint among older cats. Your vet will be able to examine the

mouth and tell you what, if anything, needs to be done about it.

● An increase in thirst could be indicative of diabetes or it could be caused by liver or kidney problems.

● Keep an eye, too, on the litter tray to make sure that the motions look healthy; if they appear too runny or too hard there could be a coeliac or intestinal problem.

● Incontinence could have a mechanical cause, such as paralysis of the bladder, but could just as easily be cystitis, which will often respond well to treatment.

● Watch for any lumps and bumps developing – they may be harmless, but monitor them for any change in shape that might indicate a tumour.

● EUTHANASIA ●

We all know that the end has to come sometime, however sad an occasion this may be. With our pets, we have the choice to save them suffering and humanely have them put to sleep.

Cats seem to have a high pain threshold, and will purr even when in great discomfort. When you have lived with your cat for many years, you will know it as well as an old friend; no matter

what pretence it puts on, you instinctively understand that all is not well and that it is unhappy. Cats hate being dirty; if a cat becomes incurably incontinent it must be feeling a miserable creature indeed. Some tumours are inoperable in advanced years, and a cat with cancer must surely suffer, whatever brave face it shows.

If you know your cat well, you will know when the time is coming – you have the ability to authorize your vet to curtail its suffering. Cats do not hold religious convictions so, when we have the opportunity to let them go in a peaceful and dignified manner, should we not do so?

ABOVE
*A small memorial
plaque in the garden
will ensure that a
much-loved pet is
never forgotten.*

SAFEKEEPING OF CATS

In today's environment there are many dangers lying in wait for the unsuspecting feline. Outside the home are cars and unguarded areas of water that could curtail at least one of a cat's nine lives. Even indoors there are dangers, not just from household appliances, but from toxic substances we use everyday, such as disinfectants and decorators' paint. Be aware of these risks and ensure your cat enjoys a long and happy life.

There are many dangers that a cat can encounter during its life. Most people consider that cats are only at risk if exposed to the great, wide world lurking outside the front door. This is simply not true: there are dangers within the home, too. Many cats allowed a free-ranging lifestyle gain a certain amount of 'street sense' and learn to look after themselves, within reason. Those living within the confines of the house rely totally on humans for their safety and wellbeing.

The decision to confine your cat to the home may be dictated by where you live. In modern towns and cities, many people live in apartment blocks where it is not always possible to let puss out for an evening constitutional. You may prefer to sleep sound in the knowledge that your cat is safe indoors. On the other hand, many people do not like the idea of fussing with indoor litter trays, and would not want a cat unless it used the garden for toilet purposes. (Consider the neighbours though – not everyone likes their flowerbeds used as cat toilets.)

Perhaps the best way to decide which way your cat will live, and the restrictions to impose upon it, is to look first at all the inherent dangers that it could meet with.

BELOW
Broken, brittle roofing panels and damaged wire mesh can constitute a real danger to any cat; these materials could pierce the skin and cause an infection to set in.

ABOVE
A well-fenced-in garden will allow your cat a little freedom without the risk of dangers from the outside world.

• OUTDOOR DANGERS •

DISEASES AND PARASITIC INFECTIONS are generally transmissible from one cat to another, so any free-ranging cat will be more prone to disease than one confined indoors. That said, these cats will acquire a certain immunity to many diseases as they are frequently exposed to low-level infections. (*See 'Health Care, Parasites, and Ailments and Illnesses' for more information.*)

FENCING AND BOUNDARIES can provide a safe area for cats as long as they are constructed in a sensible material, with no sharp barbs or other hazards. However, some people build fences to keep other people's cats out and these can be quite dangerous – electric fences and barbed wire can cause horrific damage to a domestic pet.

DOMESTIC REFUSE, left out in bins and sacks in the garden, is of great interest to any cat, not just the marauding feral. For some reason, cats seem to be especially attracted to the neighbours' leftovers. But

BELOW
*Cats love exploring,
especially in territories
that are otherwise
forbidden to them.
This cat has managed
to get itself shut in the
garden shed and might
have remained
undiscovered for some
time if the owner had
not made a habit of
checking the shed and
other outbuildings
every night.*

ABOVE
*Cats are born
scavengers and a
dislodged dustbin lid is
an open invitation.
Most food disposed of
in this way is
contaminated and, if
eaten, will give your
cat a stomach upset at
the very least.*

what goes in those bins, and what damage could it cause? Leftover food decomposes quickly, especially when the weather is warm, and if eaten could cause a severe stomach upset. Some bones, particularly from cooked chicken and rabbit, are brittle and could lodge in a cat's throat with fatal consequences. Broken glass, if not properly wrapped, can cause untold damage both externally, if trodden on and, more seriously, if swallowed. Chemicals, such as washing powder, can spill over and cause toxic problems if eaten along with waste food.

OTHER CATS. If your cat is allowed free-ranging access it will inevitably meet other cats. Most will be friendly, but an un-neutered male can be a different beast. It is not unknown for such a cat to attack a kitten.

OUTBUILDINGS may not seem danger-ous, but they are if a cat gets locked in without food and water. The time of year that poses the greatest risk is autumn, when keen gardeners do a final sweep up

of leaves, and then lock all tools away for the winter in their garden shed. This is a time for great vigilance; a cat missing at this time of year is quite often to be found locked up in a neighbour's shed. Also, look at the dangers found within a garden shed: this is usually where chemicals, paint and tools are stored, all of which are potentially dangerous to a cat, so make sure that the shed door is locked when you leave, and that no cat is inside. Make sure that outbuildings and sheds are well-maintained too – broken windows and roofing tiles are potentially hazardous.

PESTICIDES AND GARDEN SPRAYS are chemicals that many keen gardeners use, but please be careful. Anything that carries a label stating 'keep away from babies and small children' should also read 'dangerous to cats', but rarely does. Slug pellets are almost lethal to a cat. Instead,

ABOVE
Garden sheds are often used to store paint, thinners, turpentine, weedkillers and other toxic chemicals. Please make sure you keep the door firmly closed as an inquisitive cat will try to gain access, often to its own detriment.

CAT-PROOFING YOUR GARDEN

This may sound a daunting and expensive task, but need not be if your garden is reasonably small. Chicken wire or other wire mesh will do the job nicely, especially if your fences or surrounding walls are high in the first place. Using 47 mm by 50 mm (2 in by 2 in) upright batons, and the same for horizontal support across the top of the

fence, loosely attach the wire mesh so that the cat cannot get a firm grip and will be unable to jump into the neighbour's garden.

If your fence is weak or there are gaps at ground level, cover these areas right down to the ground and, if possible, bury the wire down to a level of about 150 mm (6 in).

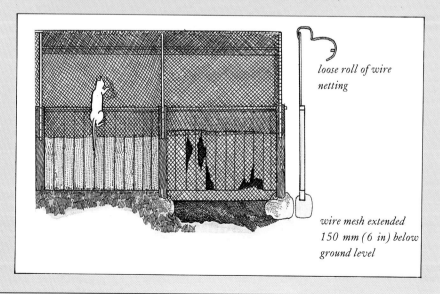

loose roll of wire netting

wire mesh extended 150 mm (6 in) below ground level

LEFT
This cat is enjoying all the benefits of a sunny garden that is beautifully maintained and weed-free; the owner is sensible and uses only environmentally friendly, cat-safe pesticides.

try using a 'slug pub' (a small container sunk in the ground and filled with beer – the slugs and snails are attracted to it and drown). For greenfly and aphids, avoid chemicals that can harm cats; diluted washing-up liquid is just as effective in killing these garden pests. Look carefully on the label of any lawn fertilizer; many contain a moss killer, and this is yet another danger. Hormone weedkillers, which encourage the plants to outgrow themselves, are the safest for animals.

ROADS AND CARS. More cats die following road accidents than from any other causes. But look on the bright side – most cats do learn from their mistakes, and few get hit by a car twice. If your cat is going to be allowed to roam free, try to give it a little advance information: in a safe container, such as a cat basket, place the cat under your car. Start the engine and rev hard (for a few seconds only, or the cat will inhale too many fumes). This should persuade the cat that a car is a

nasty animal and, hopefully, it will remember to stay well away from traffic. It is almost a case of being cruel to be kind, but it does work.

THEFT. Cats are stolen for various reasons, the main ones being vivisection and the European fur trade. A recent problem has been the increasing popularity of fighting dogs, such as pit bull terriers, and the associated rise in theft of cats used to bait the dogs before a fight. Theft poses little threat to the cat confined at home, but those allowed to wander are at risk. Try to allow your cat freedom only when you are around in the garden to supervise. Always make sure that the cat is safely back indoors before you leave the house. *Never* put your cat out at night – this is an open invitation to any would-be thief, as it is much easier to steal anything under cover of darkness. Any cat allowed outside should wear a collar with the owner's name, address and telephone number on it. Never put the cat's

BELOW
A cat allowed freedom to roam the streets is at risk both from thieves and from the possibility of a road accident.

ABOVE
Cats tend to wander around parked cars. This may seem safe but if the car was moving this photograph may have told a very different story.

● WHAT TO DO IF YOUR CAT GOES MISSING ●

● *Search your house thoroughly to make sure that the cat really is missing. It can be embarrassing to patrol the local area, telling all the neighbours that you have lost a cat, only to find the wiley creature asleep in the airing cupboard. Make sure that the cat is not accidentally shut in the bathroom, or is curled up in the linings of the curtains — another favourite hiding place.*

● *Check that the cat has not got into the neighbours' house: ask them to look particularly in warm spots, such as the bedroom, boiler room and airing cupboard. Also, ask them to check outbuildings as a frightened, lost cat will seek refuge in any dark corner.*

● *Put up notices locally, with a picture if possible, describing the cat and saying when and where it went missing. Never state anything along the lines of 'Valuable Pedigree Cat Lost', as this may encourage otherwise honest folk to keep your pet. Simply describe the way the cat looks and offer a reward for its safe return.*

● *Tell people who are up early such as the postman, milkman and paper boy. Cats revert quickly to feral habits and tend to hide in daylight, only coming out under cover of darkness to forage*

for food, so early risers are more likely to spot them.

● *If you live near a school, ask the headteacher to make an announcement. Most children are fond of pets, and will take a little extra time on their way to and from school to look out for a missing cat.*

● *Inform your local cat club, the breed club if your cat is a pedigree, local animal rescue centres, and the local veterinary practices.*

● *Put an advertisement in the 'Lost and Found' section of the local paper.*

● *Tell the police, stressing that you suspect theft of your pet. If your cat is a pedigree, this is the time to stress that it is valuable.*

● *If all else fails, try telephoning the local street cleansing department — it is better to know the ultimate fate of your cat, and it is the road cleaners who find many of the pets that have been killed on the streets.*

● *Never give up hope. Cats have been known to return home on their own accord after many months. Most cat clubs and rescue organizations link up with each other nationwide, and many missing cats eventually meet up again with their owners.*

RIGHT
Any cat allowed outside must wear a collar and tag marked with the owner's name, address and telephone number; never put the cat's name on the tag as this might encourage a would-be thief to entice a trusting feline away.

Cats are adept climbers – at least on the ascent. Coming down, especially for a young cat, is more difficult and it may need a helping hand.

LEFT
To prevent cats from climbing – and getting stuck in – trees, nail an inverted fan of wire mesh around the trunk about 2 m (6 ft) from the base.

name on as a trusting feline is more likely to go to a stranger when its name is called – and that stranger could be a cat thief.

TRAPS are rare in towns, but do pose a threat to cats in the countryside. Many traps are now illegal, but this does not prevent poachers from using them. Wherever possible, try to keep your cat in the garden, and regularly check surrounding woodlands – a prime target for trappers – for signs of traps, then inform the police who will safely remove any you find. Do not try to remove them yourself as they are very dangerous.

TREES. It is not a joke that cats get stuck in trees and the fire brigade has to be called. This is most likely to happen with kittens, so care should be shown when a young cat explores the garden; but adults can get stuck too in rescue attempts, and there is a limit to the number of times the fire brigade will come out when they have more important things to attend to. There is a simple tip to prevent cats getting caught up awkward trees: about

six feet from the ground, nail some chicken wire or similar (not barbed wire) on to the tree in a fan shape – the cat will not be able to get a firm grip to climb further, but will have enough tree to play and strop claws on.

WATER. Swimming pools, ponds, lakes and rivers are all potentially dangerous. To dispel a popular myth that cats hate water, most cats can swim, but not well and so water does constitute a danger. There are really only two options: either keep the cat away from water, or keep the water away from the cat. Cover swimming pools and ponds with cat-proof material, such as chicken wire. Large lakes, rivers and streams are more difficult to make safe; again, chicken wire can be used to fence them off. Alternatively, if this is not practicable, keep cats indoors or confined to a suitable outside run.

BELOW
A free-ranging cat will enjoy exploring the open countryside and, to a certain extent, will learn of the inherent dangers. This cat may be lying close to the river but is making no attempt to investigate the water more closely.

● CAT RUNS ●

A cat run may be another option, especially if your garden is huge, and they need not look too unsightly. Many breeders of pedigree cats have purpose-built cat houses and runs constructed in their gardens, which do look somewhat obvious. However, a small area annexed off near the house with direct access from the main building, such as through a window or door from the kitchen or back room, will allow your cat to potter in and out without any risk of theft. Make sure that it is sturdily built, using heavier wood than that suggested for cat-proofing a garden, covered in wire mesh and roofed – this is important, as otherwise the cat could climb up the wire and disappear into the world beyond. To maximize the light, use acrylic sheets, such as Perspex or Plexiglass for the roof and, again, climbing plants can be grown around the wire mesh to make the end result more pleasing to the eye. Some cat runs can look almost like little conservatories without walls.

A small cat run built adjacent to the house will provide your cat with both safety and access to fresh air.

There are possibly more dangers to be found in the kitchen than in any other single room in the house. After use the owner has thoughtfully placed an empty saucepan over the ceramic hot plate (RIGHT); this however has warmed and so the kitten has decided to curl up in the pan. A potentially more dangerous situation (BELOW), the cat investigates a pan containing boiling fish.

• INDOOR DANGERS •

Inside a nice warm house you might think that a cat is relatively safe, but is it? Take a look round your house room by room. Consider the dangers, and the associated safety precautions that you

would extend to a human toddler, and apply the same for your cat.

KITCHENS are usually the focal point of a household. Any sensible cat will want to take part in the everyday hubbub of meals being cooked, people chatting, machines whirring and above all, the warmth that exudes from this hotbed of domesticity – all cats like to feel part of the family.

Never leave pots and pans unattended. Interesting cooking smells will attract your cat, inviting it to investigate further. The result could be: at worst, a severe scald or burn; at best, your supper simply disappearing.

Hob plates, especially the ceramic variety, remain hot for some time after use. Never let a cat near these unless there is a covering lid that can be pulled over the entire hob. Failing this, place a saucepan full of cold water over the hot hob to absorb most of the heat, or keep the cat out of the kitchen until the appliance has cooled down.

Washing machines and tumble driers have some sort of fatal attraction for cats. Have you noticed how cats like to watch

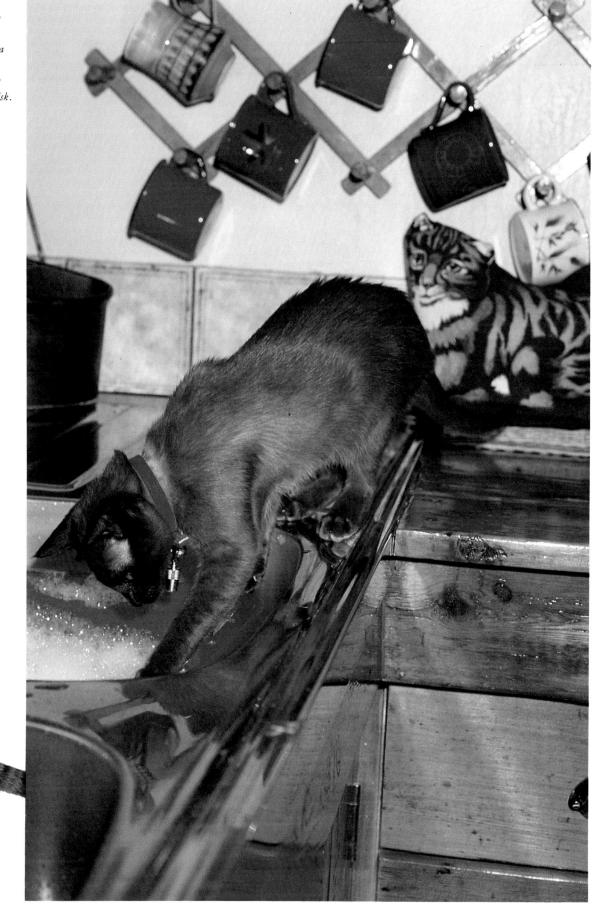

get food poisoning from dirty work surfaces. But what disinfectant do you use? Cats like to walk around the kitchen, and are probably fed in this room too, so it is hard to keep them off the work surfaces. Cats can absorb all sorts of poisons and toxins through their paw pads, and some disinfectants contain phenols and cresols which can be lethal to cats. Check the label on your disinfectant carefully. Some products do not state all their constituents; avoid these and choose one you know to be safe.

BATHROOMS. The main danger here is water, and the possibility of drowning. If you fill the bath, never leave it unattended or, if you do, make sure the bathroom door is closed so cats cannot get in. The same applies to the hand basin. A cat can be scalded badly in a hot bath so always run the cold water tap first or, if you have mixers, make sure the temperature is correct; cats move quickly and can dive for the bath before you have time to

BELOW
Cats love to sit in the kitchen and carry out their ablutions; having walked over the work surface the cat is now washing its paws. Most owners know which disinfectants are cat-friendly; be sure that the brand you buy contains no phenols or cresols.

ABOVE
Cats are fascinated by electrical appliances and will frequently try to chew through the cables, much to the annoyance of their owners. Moreover, if a cat managed to sever a mains lead it would suffer a life-threatening electric shock.

the washing going round in the machine? (Mine find the spin programme particularly interesting.) But washers can be fatal to cats. Never leave the door open, as a cat will quite happily jump in and go to sleep if the appliance is still warm. It is then so easy to throw in the laundry and switch on the machine, resulting in one very clean but very dead cat. The same applies to tumble driers which can suffocate a cat trapped inside. Make a simple house rule: never close the door and switch on the machines until a head count has been made of resident felines. Put a sticker on the door of the machines to this effect so that even visitors know the rules.

Sinks full of water can cause drowning. Although an adult cat is unlikely to drown in a kitchen sink, a small kitten could easily do so. When your sink is not in use, pull the plug or empty the bowl.

Disinfectants are part of everyday life and so they should be, especially where food is being prepared. No one wants to

RIGHT
*An open fire should
always be encased with
a fire guard.*

LEFT
*For some reason cats
seem to like dirty
laundry and will even
sleep in the laundry
basket; check your
laundry thoroughly
before putting it in the
washing machine just
in case there is a cat
lurking in the depths.*

ABOVE

Some houseplants can also present a hazard for cats; poinsettia and mistletoe, to name just two plants often found in the home, are both poisonous. Check plant guides to verify that the plants you have in the home and garden are safe.

◉ POISONOUS PLANTS ◉

There are many plants that are dangerous to cats. Some, such as laburnum seeds, are fatal if eaten, but many others can cause serious stomach upsets. Even houseplants and cut flowers can create problems. Most cats know instinctively when a plant is poisonous and will avoid it. If in doubt, contact your vet who should be able to advise you. Some cats develop allergies, in much the same way as some humans are prone to hay fever, and suffer a reaction to certain plants and trees.

A pretty picture this may seem, but remember that there may be many plants in your garden which are poisonous to cats.

close the door. There is also a danger with the toilet; many people use chemical blocks, that clean with every flush. Most of these are highly toxic, so always keep the toilet lid down if your cat has access to this room.

OTHER DANGERS lurk in every room that contains electric power points and their associated appliances. Cats, being naturally inquisitive and playful, believe that electric cables, wires and telephone leads have all been devised as cat toys, and love to chew through them. Some years ago a friend of mine spent Christmas Day resuscitating his cat after she chewed through the wire of the Christmas tree lights. The cat survived thanks to his swift actions, but not everybody knows how to effect mouth-to-nose resuscitation on a cat (*see 'Health Care'*). If your cat is a wire chewer, put special conduit over the lead of each appliance (shower hose works very well, but is a little unsightly): most electrical shops will help you.

Common household paraphernalia such as sewing boxes contain needles and pins, which can be fatal to a cat. Balls of wool and bobbins of cotton can get wound around a cat's tongue making it swell up, cause choking and, eventually, suffocation. Even the desk drawer can reveal dangers, such as rubber bands and paper clips which can harm a cat in much the same way as cotton and needles.

CHEMICALS of various kinds are kept in the home, the obvious ones being cleaning materials, but also DIY products such as glues and solvents, paint thinners, turpentine and even paint itself, all of which can be toxic. Any such substances should be kept well out of the way of cats – and children for that matter – preferably in a room or shed where they have no access.

When redecorating, *read all labels very carefully*. Nearly all modern paint products, wallpaper paste, size and wood preservatives contain fungicides and

other antibacterial agents. These can be lethal to cats. Keep cats out of rooms that are being decorated, until all fumes have disappeared. Also, because cats can absorb toxins through their paw pads – even from wallpaper paste splashes that end up on the floor – make sure that floors have been swabbed down after decorating.

OPEN WINDOWS. Cats that are confined to a flat or house need fresh air, but any worthwhile member of the feline species will soon realize how to get out of an open window, with dire consequences if it happens to be on the eighth floor. It is simple to make a wooden frame, covered with wire mesh that will fit snugly over a window frame, allowing fresh air to circulate and your cat to be safe.

BALCONIES are another problem – nice to sit out on during warm summer evenings, but your cat will want to join you and could jump over the side. Even more possible is that the cat will try to jump to any overhanging tree nearby. Again, chicken wire on a wooden frame works quite well as a deterrent – and you have the added bonus that the wire can be covered with climbing plants.

ABOVE
Some cats confined to an apartment are lucky enough to have access to a balcony or roof garden. As these are usually several storeys up it is advisable to safeguard your cat from falling by placing trellis or wire mesh around this area – if unsightly, it can be concealed with climbing plants.

BREEDING FROM YOUR CAT

*Cat breeding is a delightful, but expensive, hobby.
Few breeders actually make money from selling kittens and,
for the vast majority, cat breeding is a pleasurable pastime
and a very good way of making new, like-minded friends.
Here you will find all the necessary information on mating,
kittening and caring for the mother cat and her kittens.*

The decision to breed from your cat should be made only after careful consideration. If you have bought a pedigree cat, it will have cost you a considerable amount of money. You may have seen that the queen produced six or seven kittens, or even more, and it does not take a mathematical genius to work out that the proceeds from the sale of those kittens seem to amount to a hefty credit to the breeder's bank balance. This may tempt you to breed from your pedigree cat – although in the UK it will probably have been placed on the non-active register as many breeders discourage novices from breeding; the equivalent in the USA would be 'not for breeding' noted on the blue slip.

Or, maybe you have acquired a pretty non-pedigree cat and feel that it should be allowed to have at least one litter of kittens before being spayed.

Please think again about your reasons for wanting to breed from your cat, and consider whether you are able to afford kittens that, through your choice, have been brought into the world. Whether the cat has a pedigree as long as your arm, or is the result of an accidental mating, the resulting kittens are still living beings that will rely on you completely for a good start in life; they are *your* responsibility. Pedigree or not, they will cost you the same amount to raise, and should be given the same respect when it comes to finding suitable homes.

If you consider cat breeding a profitable business that can bring you added income with the minimum of time and effort, you are in for a shock.

BELOW
A sensible breeder will regularly weigh the kittens to ensure that they are progressing well; this mother cat obviously has other ideas.

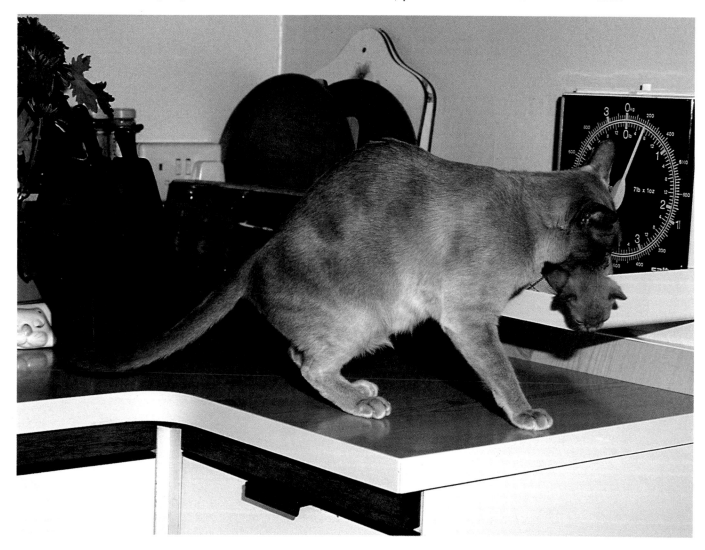

LEFT
Most usually it is the mother cat that will attend to all her kittens' needs. This family group is unusual in as much as the father is helping out too.

RIGHT
These three young Seal-point Siamese kittens clearly show the colour markings on face, ears, legs and tail expected of the breed in maturity.

RIGHT
The operation to spay a female cat is relatively quick and she will usually only need twenty-four hours to recuperate. The resulting small scar and bald patch on the flank will be only temporary.

ABOVE

Cats do make wonderful mothers, but unless there is a specific breeding programme in mind it is kinder to have the cat neutered and not add to the ever-increasing kitten population.

may come along: all of these can be reasons for a cat needing to be rehomed, and it is up to you as the breeder to assume the responsibility. Do you have the facilities to take the cat or kitten back, or will it become just another rescue statistic? And, are you knowledgeable enough to advise a prospective owner about cat health and welfare?

So, breeding cats is an expensive and demanding hobby but, given dedication to the mother cat and her offspring, it will give you many hours of pleasure. A mother cat playing with her kittens will provide far more entertainment than anything you could find to watch on the television.

Consider the expenses involved:

- Stud fee
- Testing for FeLV and other transmissible diseases
- Heating for the kittens
- Special diet for the mother cat during pregnancy and lactation
- Feeding of kittens after weaning
- Vitamin and mineral supplements
- Advertising the kittens for sale
- Stationery needed for pedigrees, and diet sheets
- Inoculations
- Registration and transfer fees

There is also the chance that there may be a hiccup in the pregnancy, kittening or weaning period, any of which will involve veterinary expenses. It is not unknown for a novice breeder to lose several kittens in the litter unless there is someone experienced available to give advice; it is possible that only one or two kittens in the first litter will survive to twelve weeks of age. This cuts down the profit margin considerably, and the breeder needs to be able to absorb these costs.

No matter how thoroughly you have checked out a prospective owner of one of your feline offspring, there is the chance that it will be returned to you. Marriages fail, houses are repossessed, a new baby

TO NEUTER OR NOT TO NEUTER

For any cat destined to become a family pet, the kindest thing to do is to neuter it. An un-neutered tom will become a nuisance not just in your own home, but also to the neighbours if it is allowed a free-ranging life. A calling

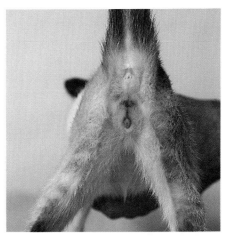

*If you are in any doubt as to the sex of your cat or kitten, consult these photographs: male (**LEFT**) and female (**BELOW**).*

queen will be just as, if not more, noisy than a male; comparable with a baby crying continuously, only louder.

Unless you have a specific breeding programme in mind, or have definite homes for all the possible kittens, neutering is the most sensible and responsible course of action.

Neutering ('altering', in the USA) is a simple operation. In the male it takes little time; an incision is made in the scrotum, each testis pulled out separately, the vas deferens severed, the testis removed, and a suture inserted. For a female, it involves abdominal surgery, but still does not take long. Usually, an incision is made about 1 cm (½ in) long on the cat's flank; in an older cat this may be done mid-line, with a longer incision straight up the underside of the belly. The ovaries and uterus are removed, and the opening stitched up. Many veterinary surgeons use dissolvable sutures, so there is no need to return to the surgery. In general, it takes only about two minutes to castrate a male, and five minutes to spay a female, so they are subjected to a minimum of anaesthetic and recover very quickly; a male will often be up and bouncing when you bring it back home, though a female may require twenty-four hours to convalesce.

It is best not to neuter your cat at too young an age; about six months is right. Neutering before this, when the endocrine system is not fully developed can cause hormonal problems, such as miliary eczema, in later life. If your kitten is female, and calls precociously, she can be given contraception, either by weekly pill or injection, until she is of a suitable size and age to undergo her operation. Male cats can be similarly precocious, and may try to mate, spray or both; if this is the case, it is better not to delay neutering.

One word of warning; cats are not hampered by morals and it is not unknown for siblings to mate each other; if you buy a pair of kittens at the same time,

watch out for signs of the female calling, or you may end up becoming a cat breeder before you would like to.

If you have decided to breed from your cat, and are sure that you will be able to find good homes for all the kittens, you must decide on a suitable stud cat.

FINDING A SUITABLE STUD CAT

The first place to start this search is with the breeder of your own cat, who will probably be able to recommend a genetically compatible sire. It is inadvisable to mate together cats that are closely related, such as mother to son or father to daughter, unless you are an experienced breeder; even then, it should really only be done to double-check that your line is not carrying deformities. Alternatively, contact the breed club who

ABOVE
Stud cats are usually housed in their own special stud quarters as most of them spray and can be somewhat anti-social within a domestic home.

should be able to give you an independent opinion of a reputable stud owner.

If possible, try not to take your maiden queen too far away for her first mating. Calling will be a new experience to her and she will be feeling a little confused; putting her in a cat carrier and driving her many miles from home will make her more upset and might cause her to come 'off call'.

When you think that you have found a suitable stud cat, go and visit the premises. Your queen will be staying there for several days, if not a week, and it is best to be sure you are happy with the stud cat, his owner, and the care, attention and accommodation offered to your female. If you are in any doubt, go elsewhere. Do not be swayed by impressive rosettes advertising the stud cat's wins; it is not always the Grand Champion that sires the best and healthiest kittens, nor his owner who will give your cat the best attention during her stay. Do not be impressed by the stud owner who has many studs available, either; stud cats are usually

housed in outside runs and, if there are several such cats available, can you be sure that they are all receiving the care that they need and, more importantly, that your cat will receive the same?

If all seems in order and you wish to proceed with the mating, the stud owner will ask you many questions.

Documents the stud owner will ask to see are:
- Pedigree certificate
- Registration document
- Inoculation certificate
- FeLV/FIV negative certificates
- Pet name of cat
- Favourite diet

A stud owner needs to know the exact parentage of a cat she or he accepts into stud; that the cat is registered in the owner's name, and that the breeder has registered it to allow for breeding. The inoculation and FeLV/FIV neg certificates assure the stud owner that risks of infections to her cat are kept to a minimum.

RIGHT
The calling queen will adopt the typical stance with her rear end raised and back legs 'paddling'.

This works both ways, and the stud owner will show you her cat's certificates too. Your cat's preferred diet and use of its pet name will also make it settle in that much more quickly.

WHEN IS YOUR CAT READY TO BE MATED?

Cats can be precocious creatures, some breeds more than others. It is not unknown for a sixteen-week-old kitten to start calling. This is far too young to contemplate a formal mating; wait until she is at least a year old.

A female cat is called a queen for good reason, which has nothing to do with royalty. It comes from the old word *quean*, meaning a whore or a hussy. When you hear your cat call, and see her pedalling her back legs and exposing her rear end, this makes sense! When your queen first comes on call, contact the stud owner and tell her. It is best to mate your cat on the second or third day of call, but an experienced stud owner may advise you to bring a novice queen to her stud as soon as possible.

The stud owner should monitor any matings and, when sure that the cats have successfully mated, ring to ask you to take the queen away. At this point, you should be given a mating certificate with all the details of the stud cat's pedigree, the dates of mating and the date on which the kittens should be born.

CARE OF YOUR CAT DURING PREGNANCY

About twenty-one days after your cat has been mated you should be able to tell if it has been successful; at this point the nipples should be slightly swollen and show a deep pink hue. If so, you have a pregnant cat on your hands and should change her diet accordingly. If you are in any doubt, your vet should be able to confirm your opinion, or contact the stud owner who will be used to dealing with pregnant cats.

As soon as you are certain that your cat is pregnant it is advisable to introduce vitamin supplements in her food; she will undoubtedly have more than one growing kitten inside her and will need all the help she can get. Calcium can be beneficial as it helps to promote the development of strong bones in the kittens. Your vet should be able to suggest various compound powders that will supply all the other additional vitamins and minerals, if

The stud cat, when
mating a queen, will
find added grip if a
mat is provided for
him. The stud cat
grasps the queen by the
scruff of her neck
(**LEFT**), and
positions the queen
squarely ready for
penetration (**BELOW**).

LEFT
The pregnant queen
will be visibly
plumper and the
nipples most apparent.

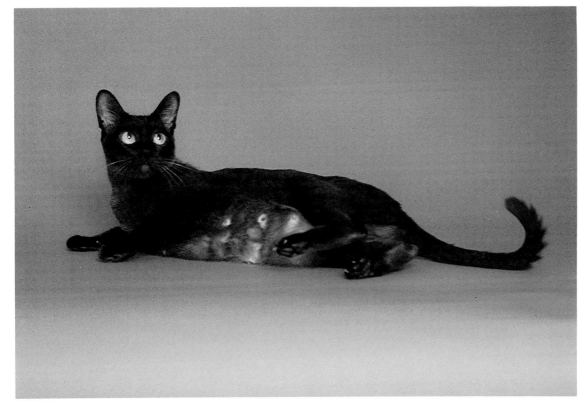

RIGHT
*This very obviously
pregnant cat is only a
day or two away from
kittening.*

RIGHT
*This very obviously
pregnant cat is only a
day or two away from
kittening.*

this is necessary, and will also tell you how long to continue giving these supplements. Many experienced breeders have found that their pregnant cats also benefit from raspberry leaf, which should be given from the fifth week of pregnancy until at least a week after kittening.

The gestation period for a cat is sixty-five days, although this may vary a day or two either side. Unless the cat seems unduly upset there is no need for panic if the cat does not produce exactly on the sixty-fifth day. A few days before the event, your cat will probably start nesting. This may not be in the place most convenient for you, and could well be in your bedroom cupboard, drawer, or linen cupboard. If possible, provide your cat with a suitable nesting box; this can be as simple as a cardboard box placed somewhere that suits you in a quiet, darkened corner. A kitten pen is ideal for containing the nest; if you are planning only one litter, you may find that the breeder of your cat will lend you one. If so, make sure you disinfect it first with a cat-friendly substance.

Line the box with alternate layers of cotton fabric and newspaper; kittening can be a messy business and it is important for the kittens to be kept as warm and dry as possible. By layering the kittening box you can remove soiled bedding after the arrival of each kitten.

◆ THE BIRTH ◆

If you are a novice breeder and have any queries or doubts before or during the birthing process, contact an experienced breeder or the owner of your cat's stud for advice. Don't call the vet at this point; not all vets are cat breeders and therefore see only problematic births. However, it is likely that all will go well and according to plan. Most cats find kittening easy, and have no problem delivering their litter efficiently.

The first sign of impending birth will be 'a bubble' appearing outside the vulva

– this is the bulging bag of waters; at this point the waters will burst and the cat should be visibly contracting. Cats are designed for multiple births, unlike humans; this means they have several, small babies, not one huge one, and so in general have an easier time. Most cats will purr all through the delivery and will only rest when all the kittens are safely born. It is always as well to be prepared to act as midwife and you should be prepared to have *clean* towels (or kitchen roll), blunt-tipped scissors and a bowl of boiled water handy in case your cat needs assistance.

Cats usually know exactly what to do, but an inexperienced maiden queen can get confused; she should bite through the umbilical cord, releasing the kitten from its placenta, and wash the kitten thoroughly with her raspy tongue to stimulate the circulation. This does not always happen and you may have to cut through the umbilical cord and stimulate the kit-

ABOVE

A kitten box makes an ideal nesting area. Before the birth, line the base with alternate layers of cotton fabric and newspaper and provide soft, warm bedding once the kittens have arrived.

ten yourself. Cut about 4 cm (1½ in) from the kitten, and remember to squeeze the cord immediately below the point at which it is severed to stem the blood flow and help the end of the cord to clot and close. Then, rub the kitten vigorously.

If the kitten does not appear to be breathing, you must take immediate action. It is likely that it has water in its lungs from inhaling the amniotic fluid, and this must be expressed quickly. Take the kitten in your hand, grasping it firmly, and using your index finger as support for its head with a motion similar to an over-arm cricket throw, swing the kitten firmly (but do not let go). This

should get rid of any fluid in the lungs.

Each kitten is attached to its own placenta, which has at this point served its main purpose – to supply nutrition to the kitten while still in the womb. The placenta now has a different function, which is to supply a quick, nutritious meal for the mother cat which will stimulate the supply of milk. Although at least one placenta should be eaten, it is not necessary for her to eat them all. Some years ago a well-intentioned novice breeder rang me to say that his cat had eaten all her placentas; she had apparently given up after the second one and so the owner gently sautéed the remaining six in a little butter and garlic to make a temp-

KITTENING

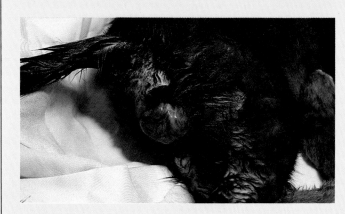

A kitten, still encased in its amniotic sac, is being delivered.

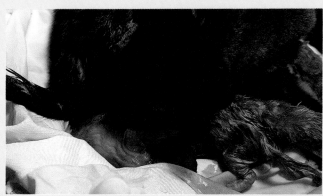

The mother chews through the umbilical cord.

The mother cat's raspy tongue not only helps to clean and dry the newborn kittens, but also acts as a stimulus to encourage circulation.

The proud mother with her family of five a couple of days after the birth.

⦿ NO CAUSE FOR ALARM ⦿

Some of the processes of birth may seem a little disturbing if you have never seen them before, but they are all perfectly normal and are no cause for alarm. The general pattern of kittening involves some messy stages:

⦿ Shortly before the birth of the first kitten a plug of mucus will come away. Even if this happens as early as a week before the kittening is due, do not worry unless the mucus has an unhealthy greenish hue or blood is discharged.

⦿ Kittening is a stressful experience and it is not uncommon for a kitten to suffer foetal distress; this is equally common in human babies and usually simply means that the force of delivery causes the bowels to empty and faeces to be expelled.

⦿ Birth is a bloody business, do not be distressed by the amount of red-tinged secretions that will be seen. The mother may continue oozing in this manner for a few days. If the colour changes, or the discharge becomes more profuse, contact the vet immediately as this could indicate a life-threatening infection to both mother and kittens.

ting breakfast for her. This is perhaps taking things a little too far!

It is sometimes possible for a maiden to confuse a kitten with placenta, in which case she may try to eat the kittens and suckle the afterbirth; this is why it is important to monitor your cat's kittening in case she makes a mistake.

It is helpful to make a list itemizing each kitten's time of birth and sex, and checking that each birth was accompanied by a complete placenta. This last point is important because the afterbirth may not be expelled immediately. Any afterbirth retained within the mother can cause serious infection. If in doubt, contact your vet immediately.

The whole procedure could take as little as an hour or could last half a day. Unless your cat seems ill at ease there is no cause to worry; let nature take its course. If she seems to strain, or a kitten appears stuck, it is wise to contact your vet or the stud owner, either of whom should be able to give you advice.

⦿ AFTERCARE OF KITTENS ⦿

For the first few weeks the mother will supply all the kittens' needs. She will feed them, wash them and keep them warm. At about ten days or so the kittens will open their eyes and will start taking an interest in the world outside their nest. By the time they are about three weeks old they will be wanting to venture farther afield. At this age it is sensible to warn your family to watch where they step, as it is all too easy to curtail a small kitten's life with a hefty blow from a foot. (This is where a kitten pen comes into its own.) From the moment they become mobile until they are ready to leave your home when they are twelve weeks old, you must be on a constant vigil.

The kittens will become more and more inquisitive and by the time they are four or five weeks old they will be willing to lap food. The best weaning foods are those prepared for human babies, but minced chicken or fish is usually quite acceptable; pilchards are excellent as they smell strong and encourage the kittens to eat, but only give them small amounts to whet their appetites as it is a very rich food.

By the time kittens are six weeks old they should be able to eat regular cat foods. It is important that you get your kittens used to a varied diet of different brands so they do not become faddy eaters in later life.

At about ten weeks your kittens will be

Continued page 102

KITTEN DEVELOPMENT

LEFT
Kittens are born with their eyes sealed and will do little for the first few days other than suckle and sleep.

BELOW LEFT
At about ten days old the kitten's eyes will open.

BELOW RIGHT
At about three weeks old the ears will assume an upright position, making the kitten look more like a miniature version of the adult cat it will become.

RIGHT
By the time the kittens are six weeks old they should be weaned and happy to eat solid food.

BELOW RIGHT
Under strict supervision, ten-week-old kittens are ready to explore the garden for the first time.

BOTTOM
Twelve weeks old, fully inoculated and weaned, these youngsters are now ready to go to their new homes.

ready for the first of their two inoculations. This is a straightforward procedure but the occasional kitten may suffer an adverse vaccine reaction. This is not serious and will probably only cause the affected kitten to be slightly unwell for a day or two, possibly with the odd snuffle or sneeze. For this reason it is always advisable to keep the kittens for three or four days after they have been inoculated, to allow for recovery, before letting them go to their new homes.

ANTISOCIAL HABITS IN KITTENS

Kittens are often preoccupied with faecal matter. This can be displayed in one of two ways.

They may become overly interested in their cat litter to the point where they try to eat it. This is often because the litter tray is too clean; always leave a little urine-soaked litter in the tray after changing it. This should encourage the kitten to realize what the tray has been put down for. Or, forget the idea of using litter at all, and substitute torn or shredded paper until the kitten has realized the tray is for toilet purposes. If the kitten ingests cat litter, particularly a wood-based variety, this will swell in the stomach and could cause a blockage which would require veterinary treatment.

Although it is unusual, some kittens are 'dirty' and this is an exceedingly hard habit to break. Once such behaviour has been initiated by one kitten it is not unusual for the whole litter to follow suit. The most common reason is that the litter tray is not clean enough and so the kittens feel the need to defecate elsewhere. It is possible to buy cat repellents but you should not use these where very young kittens are in the house. One tip: cats and kittens do not like eating in an area that has been soiled, so try putting the food bowls over the preferred spot for defecation and you should find that the problem is overcome very quickly. If the place is

inaccessible to food bowls, try covering it with tin foil or plastic sheeting; few cats like the sound of their excrement falling onto these surfaces.

SELLING YOUR KITTENS

If you already have suitable homes lined up, invite the prospective owners to visit the kittens frequently. The kittens will not be fully inoculated until they are twelve weeks old and so visitors must be subjected to strict hygiene procedures. Always get them to wash their hands with a disinfectant solution before handling the young kittens. Early handling by the new owners is important as this will give them the opportunity to form a bond with the kitten that is to become a part of their household.

If your cat has produced more kittens than you have homes for, you may need to advertise. Most breed clubs offer the service of a kitten list and this is a good place to start – the prospective buyer has at least gone to the bother of finding out about the relevant breed club. You can also advertise in local papers and specialist cat magazines. From these sources the purchasers are an unknown entity and it is up to you to question them thoroughly to ensure their suitability (*see 'Where to Find a Cat and How to Choose One'*).

ABOVE
Most kittens will instinctively know what the litter tray is for and will not need to be house-trained.

LEFT
Kittens love to play and explore new areas; although the hob unit was switched off and cold, it is inadvisable to encourage kittens to play in the kitchen where many dangers lurk.

PROBLEMS DURING BREEDING

There are just a few problems that can affect either the mother cat or her kittens during the early weeks. Don't be unduly alarmed by these descriptions, but observe your charges closely so prompt action can be taken, if necessary.

*Sometimes, a mother cat is unable to supply all the milk her kittens need, especially if it is a large litter; with a family of four (**BELOW**) she is unlikely to have any problems. Occasionally, mastitis may also prevent the cat from feeding her young. Kittens can fare well if foster fed with evaporated milk diluted with water (see Lack of Milk), as this healthy youngster demonstrates (**RIGHT**).*

LEFT
*If for whatever reason the mother is unable to feed her kittens, this specially designed kitten foster feeder bottle will enable you to provide the kittens with the nourishment they need. (*See Lack of Milk, below.)

• INTUSSUSCEPTION •

DESCRIPTION

This is not common and is a bowel disorder where the intestine doubles back on itself in telescopic fashion, causing an obstruction. The symptoms are lack of appetite and no evidence of stools being passed, because the intestine is blocked.

ACTION

In a minor case it is possible to operate and remove the offending portion of bowel; in a compound case the prognosis is not good and the affected kitten will probably have to be humanely destroyed by your vet.

• LACK OF MILK •

DESCRIPTION

In general, mother's milk is generated by supply and demand; if the kittens are not hungry or indeed well enough to wish to suckle, the mother's supply of milk will dry up. Mastitis (*see right*) is another cause of this. In a very large litter the mother may not have enough milk to go round.

ACTION

If the litter is large, you will need to rotate the kittens, then top up with a foster feeder bottle containing evaporated milk diluted one part milk to three parts cooled boiled water. Proprietary cat milk substitutes are available but they can sometimes cause constipation in small kittens.

• MASTITIS •

DESCRIPTION

Mastitis usually affects the lactating queen. The symptoms are of general ill health, and the most obvious sign is that one or several of the mammary glands is impacted and feels hot and lumpy to the touch. The danger here, if the queen is still suckling, is that the kittens will drink infected milk and so suffer a form of poisoning.

ACTION

It is important to ensure that the kittens do not suckle from an infected gland; you can do this by bandaging over the affected nipple, but your vet will advise the best course of action. It is also important to get the queen to the vet as soon as possible, for a confirmed diagnosis, advice, and prescription of a suitable course of antibiotics.

• PYOMETRA •

DESCRIPTION

This can affect a cat at any age but is more likely to occur after kittening. It is an infection of the uterus and is most commonly indicated by a thick, creamy secretion from the vulva.

ACTION

In mild cases it can be treated with antibiotics but if severe, it requires the removal of the reproductive organs – that is, the cat has to be spayed.

HEALTH CARE

Cats are generally healthy creatures but they will benefit from annual inoculations and health-checks. Inoculations are extremely important to safeguard cats from certain feline diseases, but there are many illnesses and ailments from which you cannot protect your cat in this way. Yet, by following a routine system of care, any changes in your cat can be immediately detected and veterinary diagnosis and treatment sought. Accidents can happen, too, and this chapter covers all these aspects of cat ownership, advising on symptoms, what action to take and treatment.